ADVANCED PRAISE FOR
GETTING THE MONEY

I LOVE *Getting the Money* by Susan Lassiter-Lyons. If you need to raise private money to fund your real estate deals and don't know where to start this book is just what you need. I know – I'm living proof. Using the strategies Susan teaches I was able to raise just shy of $1M in less than 90 days. Talk about cutting months off my learning curve. This is definitely one of the best books I have ever read on raising private money. I can't imagine how it could have been written any better or how it can be any more helpful unless Susan raises the money for you ;)

Bill Walston, www.billwalston.com

Susan Lassiter-Lyons's new book is everything you want in a great business book. It's tremendously useful: the information therein can make financing your projects both easier and more profitable. It's compelling: using personal stories and examples, Susan has created a business book that is actually fun to read, which is a rarity. It's inspiring: Susan's book will get your entrepreneurial motor running and inspire you to take your business beyond anything you thought possible. The information is so valuable, it's worth many times what she's charging for it. I suggest you buy it and devour it immediately.

Kriss Bergethon, www.legendven.com

Susan nailed it with the simplest approach to tapping in to MILLIONS. For anyone who dares to live life to the fullest, and who wants to raise endless cash for deals (while keeping full control of the process) – this is THE approach to take.

Mark Evans, DM, DN, www.markevansdm.com

Financing a real estate deal is hard in today's world, or at least that's what I thought. Getting the Money lays out the steps you need to follow to make your deal happen. And even better, the book is fun to read!

Diane Kennedy, CPA, New York Times best-selling author of Loopholes of the Rich and other books, Ustaxaid.com

GETTING
THE
MONEY

The Simple System for Getting Private Money for Your Real Estate Deals

SUSAN LASSITER-LYONS

THOMAS NOBLE BOOKS

Permissions Department
Thomas Noble Books
427 N Tatnall Street #90946
Wilmington, DE 19801-2230

This publication is designed to provide accurate and authoritative information in regard to the subject matter covered. It is sold with the understanding that the author is not engaged in rendering professional services. If legal, accounting, medical, psychological, or any other expert assistance is required, the services of a competent professional person should be sought.

Library of Congress Control Number: 2014921317

ISBN: 978-1-934509-77-7

Printed in the United States of America

Editing by Ben McColm and Gwen Hoffnagle

Cover design by 2faceddesigns.com

DEDICATION

Getting the Money is dedicated to my uncle and honorary dad,
William H. Lassiter Jr., for blazing the trail of entrepreneurship in
our family and being my beacon on that trail.

ACKNOWLEDGEMENTS

This book was born over great food and pinot noir on a night too cold for flip-flops. However, it wouldn't be my book if fun and teamwork were not involved. Let me give special thanks to:

Ben McColm and Gwen Hoffnagle for their editorial genius and for saving me from the wrath of the grammar and spelling correctors of the world.

Lynne Klippel of Thomas Noble Books, who encouraged me to write this book and kept the project moving with her talented team of editors and designers.

Ed Warman for opening my eyes to the world of private money.

Annette Gonzales for 15 amazing years.

And, most important, to my students, who have implemented this system to grow their real estate businesses, improve neighborhoods, and provide housing to thousands worldwide.

TABLE OF CONTENTS

CHAPTER ONE: Bridging the Gap   9

CHAPTER TWO: Mapping the Plan, or Planning the Map?   19

CHAPTER THREE: Unmasking Your Secret Identity   31

CHAPTER FOUR: Creating Your Program; "It Lives! It Lives!"   41

CHAPTER FIVE: Building Your Team   55

CHAPTER SIX: Where's the Money?   65

CHAPTER SEVEN: Stranger Marketing   77

CHAPTER EIGHT: The Presentation   87

CHAPTER NINE: The Psychology of the Presentation   97

CHAPTER TEN: Closing the Deal   109

CHAPTER ELEVEN: Tending the Garden; Managing
Your Private Money Partners   119

CHAPTER TWELVE: The Complexity of Commitment   131

Case Studies from People Who Used the Getting
the Money System   141

About Susan   149

Hey, Susan, How Can You Help Me?   150

Getting the Money

Chapter One

BRIDGING THE GAP

"Today, I will translate the reality of my dreams into my ordinary day for extraordinary results."

–Mary Anne Radmacher

The Reality of Your Dreams

I have a saying on the wall beside my bed. Every morning when I open my eyes the first thing I see is, "Today I will translate the reality of my dreams into my ordinary day for extraordinary results."

What that says to me is pretty profound. Not every day has to be spectacular. This saying reminds me to keep my dreams in front of me at all times, even though it seems like I'm stuck in the minutiae of my business. And even though it seems like I'm spinning in the administrative part that I just hate, I know that I have my eye on the ultimate prize. Everything I'm doing during my ordinary day is making my dreams come true. Write it down; it's pretty powerful.

I'm honored that you're taking the first step in translating your dreams with me, but let's talk about why you're reading this book. You're here because there's a gap. Wherever you are in your business, there's a gap that you're trying to bridge; a gap from where you are to where you want to be. Whether you are someone already investing in real estate but looking to increase your buying capacity, or you're looking to ride the investment train but just have no idea where to get a ticket, you have a goal, right? You have a dream; something that you're trying to achieve. That's the reason you've taken this first step toward real change.

The Two Speed Bumps

I think there are just two things that keep us from achieving our dreams in real estate investing. The biggest, by far, is lack of funding. It's hard to close any investment deal with empty pockets. We're going to fix that. My vision for you is to raise $1 million in private money for your real estate business. Sound impossible? I'm going to teach you exactly how to raise that much – and more – regardless of your credit score, regardless of your experience, and regardless of your doubts. As you go through this book, I ask only two things of you. Be committed to this process, and step outside your comfort zone. It's always scary when you put yourself out there. Fear is the second thing that keeps us from achieving our dreams, and unless you trust and take those first few scary steps, you'll be stuck in the same place you find yourself today. Remember, insanity is doing the same thing over and over and expecting a different result. It's time to break that cycle.

Conventional Financing

Our problem is that bank financing is nearly impossible. Conventional bank financing from the Bank of Americas and the Wells Fargos of the world is real tough to get. Fannie Mae (Federal National Mortgage Association) and Freddie Mac (Federal Home Loan Mortgage Association), the overseers of these conventional mortgages, have implemented some crazy rules. They set up these rules so they can package the loans they write and underwrite and then sell them off in giant pools to secondary markets. Millions and billions of dollars' worth of loans are sold to Wall Street buyers.

But Wall Street doesn't want to deal with all the variations like "This is an interest-only loan, this one is a second mortgage, this one is eight percent, and this one four percent." They want to homogenize everything and they want it all to conform. That's why they imposed these rules of conventional financing like "no refinances within 120 days to a year." This one makes it super-tough for people who are using hard money to finance rehabs, doesn't it? How about the rule that restricts the number of properties owned to a maximum of ten; this one I've never really understood. If the properties are cash-flowing, why can't you have an unlimited number of properties financed? The rule that restricts stated income loans hurts a lot of us who are self- employed, right? We have to go into a kind of two- to three- year hiding period so that we can pay ourselves a W-2 salary and build up the history the conventional lenders want to see. There are many more, along with some crazy hoops that we just don't want to jump through!

Another option for funding your deals is to get financing from the hard-money lenders, but they are too greedy. I can say that because I was one. We ran a loan program that was four points and 15 percent interest because that's what the market would bear. It was a great loan program, too, but not practical for long- term investment financing.

Solving the Problem with Private Equity

Here's how you solve the problem: You create and you control the funding for your deals. You set the rates and decide the terms, and you decide who will be lucky enough to partner with you. This is a mindset issue, and I want this to sink in, so I'm going to say it again: You get to decide who is going to be lucky enough to partner with you. The leaders in this industry have mastered creative financing and raising capital, so we're going to be talking about the real plum: private equity.

Private equity consists of investors and hedge funds that make investments directly into private companies. We all have private real estate companies or can easily set up an investment company. Individual investors and institutional investors provide capital for private equity. In 2012 a total of $347 billion was raised to invest in 2,083 companies in the United States, some of which were real estate companies just like yours.

Relationship Financing

I love watching the show Shark Tank. The gist of the show is entrepreneurs and inventors stand in front of five investors (the sharks) and pitch their company, idea, or product. Then they tell the sharks what they are willing to give up so that one or more of the sharks will invest in them. What's interesting to me is the reaction of the sharks. Often somebody will go in there with a great idea that's already making money for their company, but the sharks reject them saying, "We hate you, and we're not going to work with you." Then some joker comes in and says, "Hey, here's my idea, and we're pre-revenue," which is just a fancy way of saying, "We're not making any money because we don't know how," and the sharks jump all over it because they like the guy. This bias happens every day in the real world.

Real estate investing is a relationship business. When we're talking about private money and funding for your business, I call it "relationship financing." When people genuinely like you, feel like they're in alignment with you, think that you might be fun to hang around, and they might be able to make some money – that's when the magic happens. Private money is simply that – using private money partners to fund deals. Everybody else in the business calls them private money lenders, or just private lenders. My vernacular is a bit different because I like to think of them as much more than that. I like to treat them as partners. Those partners can invest in your company and your deals in one of two ways. They can be debt investors who make you a loan and collect a set amount of interest each month, or they can be equity investors who get a percentage of the cash flow or a percentage of the equity in your deal or your company. We'll talk more about this differentiation in a little while.

What the Survey Says

When I teach this material at my seminars and workshops, I survey the audience to help me understand their specific needs in growing their investment businesses. One of the questions on the survey is always, "If lack of funding is the main thing that's keeping you from being successful in your real estate investing business, what is stopping you from going out and raising private money for your deals?" Do you know what the number one answer is? Drumroll, please: "*I don't know where to start.*" For most people, the number one constraint is they just don't know where to start, whom they should talk to, or what they should say. We're going to take care of all that.

The next-most-popular answer is: "*I don't know anyone with any money.*" This one drives me nuts. There was $347 billion up for grabs last year. Somebody's got some money!

Finally: *"I don't know how to structure the deals."* That one can be a little scary when you're not sure of your numbers and you're not sure what you can afford to pay your investor. You don't want to pay them too much and then make your deal unprofitable, but you don't want to pay them too little and risk having them bail on you when it comes time for the next deal.

The Proof Is in the Pudding; My Results

It would be easy for someone to speculate about how to raise private funds and how to structure deals in ways that should work, and then write a book about it. But everything I'm going to teach you in this book comes from personal experience. I have been investing in real estate since 1994 and have been practicing the techniques in this book since 2004. You're going to get the benefit of all my trial and error and how I figured all this stuff out, and end up with a plan that works. How do I know it works? Let me tell you about my results.

Since 2004 I've raised $26.2 million in private money. I've been able to leverage that money to $400,000 in hedge-fund and syndication fees, ownership interest in 740 units nationwide, a five- figure monthly cash flow, and a seven-figure net worth. I can now just trade my expertise for ownership in projects because I'm able to bring in money. It's huge, but not necessarily typical.

But what if you only accomplished one-tenth of what I've accomplished – and I'm nobody special? One-tenth would be

$2.6 million. Would $2.6 million change your business or your life? If you had a blank check for $2.6 million to pay cash for whatever deal you wanted – to put together your own hedge fund, buy up non-performing notes, buy a package of foreclosed properties, or invest in an apartment building – would that change your life? It changes your life. I know firsthand because it changed mine.

Don't Love the Car; Love Where It's Taking You

I know that you're reading this because you want to bridge the gap from where you are to where you want to be. The bottom line is that real estate investing is just a vehicle to get you where you really want to be and help you achieve what you really want to achieve. It goes back to "The Reality of Your Dreams." Nobody is in love with real estate. You don't daydream in school when you're growing up thinking, "If only I could get a rental." But you do think, "If only I could go to Bora Bora and vacation in one of those cool huts over the ocean." That has a very different feel to it. You don't have to love the car, just love where you're going. I want you to give this some thought because it's important to know why you're doing this. I'm going to give you a plan to get you where you need to be – to bridge that gap. But you have to understand why you are on this road to begin with and why you chose real estate investing as your vehicle to get you there.

There are lots of different ways to make money. Watch Shark Tank and you'll see six in one show. What I want you to do is take two minutes right now and write down your answer to this question: What is your big, over-arching dream? What is that one big goal that you want to achieve – the whole reason you want to bridge that gap from where you are to where you want to be?

Free at Last, Free at Last

When I did this exercise, the reality of my dreams was freedom. I'm a firm believer that just about any dream you can think of comes down to freedom – time freedom, financial freedom, or some other form of freedom. As human beings we don't like to be constrained. My answer was, "I want to do what I want, when I want, where I want, with whomever I want."

The income that my company generates is not necessarily dependent on me. In fact, I've set up my systems and processes so well that my company usually makes more money when I'm out of the way. Sometimes the biggest constraint in my business is me because I'm in there mucking everything up. I hear, "Would you just get out of here so everything would go back to normal?"

So now my focus is travel. I wanted to go to Ireland and spend a significant amount of time there because I'm Irish on both sides. I also wanted to go to Dominican Republic because I heard it was beautiful; that the ocean there was just amazing. I even wanted to get a beach house and summer on Cape Cod. So in the last fourteen months, "check," "check," "check," I've done all three of those things. It's a testament to this program.

I want you to translate the reality of your dreams into your ordinary day for extraordinary results. It means that you're not working toward the next real estate deal, but toward your over-arching dream, whatever it is – time freedom, financial freedom, travel, put the kids through college, stay at home, or put the kids in an RV and travel around all year. Whatever that dream is, that's the reason you're doing this.

Your Secret Identity

When you introduce yourself to new people and you tell them what you do for a living, what do you tell them? Do you tell them you're a real estate investor, or do you say you do that "other" job? A lot of us have a secret identity. If you've ever seen my office, it's covered in Wonder Woman everything. Yes, I even have a Wonder Woman mug. Alas, my secret identity has been revealed, and it turns out I'm a real estate investor. Perhaps I'm both. You never know.

When I first started investing, I was a Hertz rent-a-car employee. For so long I kept my real estate investing identity a secret from my family, my friends, and my coworkers because I was the Hertz girl. I went to work for the car-rental industry when I was a sophomore in college, at nineteen years old. I worked for Dollar rent-a-car for five years and Hertz for eleven. I worked my way up the ladder and found myself in Park Ridge, New Jersey, at the Hertz corporat headquarters, and I hated it; absolutely hated it. I started real estate investing on the side, but I didn't tell anybody. That's a big problem if you're trying to raise private money for your deals. It's a problem if you're the Hertz girl and you go to your Uncle Bill and say out of left field, "Hey Uncle Bill! I've got this project that I want to do. It's a rehab – a duplex in Aurora, Colorado – and I'm just going to need a $180,000 investment from you, okay?" "How about, um… no." I created a credibility problem for myself because I didn't let people know what I was doing. I didn't share my identity with them; that I was a real estate investor first and foremost.

Your identity is a big part of what you need to get right in your life if you want to start systematically building the credibility you want and need to have in order to do this successfully.

I want to challenge you to share details about your real estate deals when you meet people and when you interact with your family. If they look at you weird like, "I thought you were bossing around those car-rental guys? What's this with the duplex now?" say, "Let me explain to you what I'm doing. I'm doing both, and here's how I'm making that work." Invite people into your business. Share your successes with them. Share your challenges with them. They'll get on your side. The people who know you and love you want to help you, but they can't help if they don't know what you're doing.

Not Part Time, Not Full Time, but BIG Time

There are three ways you can do this business. You can do it part time, and that's fine. That's how I started. You can do it full time. Or you can do it BIG time. Whether you're doing this part time or fifty hours a week, I want to challenge you to forget about the part-time/full-time thing and just to commit to BIG time. I am not driving you to your destination; I'm offering you the keys to the car. Are you ready? Good. Let's get started!

Chapter Two

MAPPING THE PLAN, OR PLANNING THE MAP?

> *"All the world's a stage and most of us are desperately unrehearsed."*
>
> – Sean O'Casey

Let's talk about your business plan. I want you to start thinking about your real estate investing venture as a business. Businesses have divisions, and in my experience the divisional framework I'm about to teach you is ideal for this industry. Below are the divisions you can have in your investment company and some of the supporting cast.

Your Business Divisions

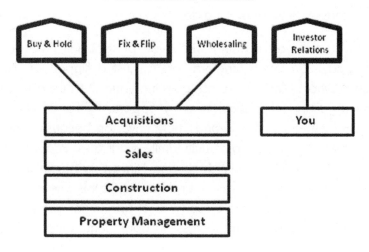

Business Divisions; Your Company's Split Personality

First up in terms of divisions is a *buy-and-hold division*. That's the area from which you manage your purchased properties, keeping them for a predetermined amount of time. Often these are rental properties you hold, realizing a degree of equity until the market bears a better return and it's time to unload them.

Next is a *fix-and-flip division*, in which you hold your purchased properties until rehabilitation work is complete. Then you resell them at a markup for a greater profit margin.

The next division is *wholesaling* – when you purchase distressed properties, often in quantity, and then flip them to other wholesalers or rehabbers for a relatively small markup. What wholesaling lacks in large, single-deal profits it makes up for in volume.

The *investor relations division* is dedicated to finding, creating, and nurturing your relationships with those who fund your projects. Most of what I will be teaching you lands squarely in the investor relations division because, as I pointed out in the first chapter, no money – no deal.

Here's what you're doing when you put yourself in a box and say, "I'm just a landlord" or "I'm just a flipper" or "I'm just a wholesaler": You're not allowing yourself to be able to leverage and capitalize on every opportunity. For example, I am essentially a buy-and- hold investor because what I'm investing in now are multi-family syndicates. People put together big multi-family deals and I invest money in them, usually as a passive investor, and I make returns. The people I invest with are seeking these kinds of apartment deals, and occasionally they'll come across an apartment complex that isn't quite worthy of our investment team. Maybe it's a C- class building or fixer-upper – something that needs a lot of work and not what we want to hold in our portfolio long term. If we have a construction team, though, we can put some work into that apartment building and then flip it or put it into our buy-and-hold division. Being diverse gives you more opportunity to turn almost any deal into profit.

As you generate leads for either your buy-and-hold division or your fix-and-flip division, you will come across deals that you don't want to do. That is why you should consider having a wholesaling division; it's just another way to monetize those leads that you get.

Support Teams; Rounding Up Your Posse

Once you establish your buy-and-hold division, your fix-and-flip division, your wholesaling division, and your investor relations division, assemble four support teams to help you. Your acquisitions team should consist of just one VIP: you. You should be the one out there getting the deals, acquiring the properties, and writing the offers. You could also have a realtor on your team, and could have an assistant who, well… assists.

Your sales team will help you dispose of the properties you've acquired. You can have a listing realtor to help you manage dispositions. You can also have someone in house who flips those deals to wholesalers.

A *construction team* is a must if you're rehabbing. There is nothing so painful and time-consuming to a rehabber than finding and assembling a whole new construction team every time they do a rehab project. It stinks. It's much better to put a good team together once and continue to work with that team over and over and over. As trusted partners, you will grow together and get better together, and you will both know and understand each other's expectations for every project.

You will need a *property management team* to manage your buy- and-hold division. You should not self-manage your properties, even if you only have one. You need a property manager. My motto is, "You hire for where you want to be, not where you are." I've had two businesses that I founded from the ground up. One of them was a multiple-six-figure business, and my current one hit seven figures in August of 2013. Hire for where you want to go, not for where you are, because without a team to support you it will be very difficult to get there.

Your Investor Relations Division: A Team of One

Your investor relations division is to identify, introduce, and invest with your private money partners, and manage that process. It is you. You cannot outsource this division. One of the biggest questions I get is, "I need about a million dollars; can I hire somebody to raise the money for me?" Um, good luck with that! That is your baby. It's your division.

Now we're going to look at how to take the lead in your investor relations division, what tools you need, and how to implement the strategy of "identify, introduce, and invest."

It all flows like this:

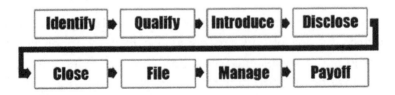

You identify the prospects, you qualify the prospects, and you introduce your opportunity to them. Then you make some form of disclosure about what you're going to be using the money for and what the risks are for them. You close the deal, file the paperwork, and manage the property and your investment partners. When the deal pays off, then you're off to the next one. That is the flow for every deal.

Company Goals; Are We There Yet?

What are the goals of your real estate investment company? What is it that you're trying to accomplish? It's not just one deal. You have objectives. What are your investment criteria? In what specifically do you invest? How much do you need? What rate of return can you afford? Who are your ideal partners? Can you accomplish your goals with one partner or do you need a group?

Before you put the car in drive, you first have to figure out the goals of your real estate company and your investment criteria. Without those two fundamental pieces you'll never be able to raise a penny because you'll never be able to communicate to anybody what the heck it is you're doing.

It's the old S.M.A.R.T. goals – specific, measurable, attainable, relevant, and time-bound. When somebody pitches to me but can't clearly articulate what the goals of their real estate investing company are, do you think I'm going to give them my money? No way! I think, "This guy doesn't know what he's doing." So at a high level you need to figure out what the goals are for your real estate company.

The following is an example of a ten-year plan: "My goals and objectives are to acquire, rehab, and rent forty distressed properties. I'm going to acquire one property every three months; that's four per year for ten years. I will finance with private money and repair, rent, and refinance properties that are below eighty percent loan-to-value. I will refinance at seven percent interest on a fifteen-year fixed term, reinvest as much cash flow as possible in the form of extra payments to accelerate the loan payoffs, and after only ten years I will have captured two-point-three million in equity while generating thirteen thousand in positive cash flow per month." That sounds like a plan I can get behind! Does your plan sound anything like this?

The One-Page Business Plan; Simple Is Smart

I'm not a big fan of giant business plans. I had a guy proudly approach me at an event and say, "Susan, I'm so excited. I just got my business plan finished for my company." I said, "That's awesome! How long did it take you?" He said, "I didn't do it. I paid a guy eight thousand dollars to write it for me." Wow. Why on earth would he do that? Just as I'm trying to impress upon you that you cannot outsource the creation and the management of your investment division, who do you think the best person would be to write the business plan for your own business? It's you. It's not someone you find on Craigslist who will just copy one from the internet or do a software fill-in-the-blank and charge you eight grand. You're the one who needs to figure this out.

I like the *one-page business plan*. Here's how you do it: Start with your business vision. Write down your value and mission statements. Set clear objectives. Lay down your strategies and spell out your plan. The mission statement for all my companies has always been: "Have fun. Create value." I have it on my business cards. It's painted on the wall of our office. And if anybody ever asks, I always say, "That's right – and the fun comes first for a reason." Why bother doing it if it's not fun?

My value statement is very different. Your value statement is your answer when somebody asks, "What do you do?" I usually say, "I put together lucrative real estate deals so my partners make safe, consistent profits." When I say that to someone, they want to know more 100 percent of the time. I've never had anybody say, "Oh, that's nice," and turn and walk away. They always say, "Really? How do you do that?" Then you get the opportunity to share what you're doing.

This all speaks to revealing your secret identity. Next time you're hanging out at a family thing and someone asks you, "What are you up to? How many cavities did you fill last week?" (if you're also a dentist, for example) that's not what you're going to talk about, right? You're going to say, "I'm working on a real estate opportunity and I'm looking for partners who want to make safe, consistent profits." How might that change the paradigm?

Here's what a one-page business plan might look like for a wholesaling business:

VISION

Within the next three years, grow My Wholesaling Business, LLC, into a $500,000 annual revenue real estate company that specializes in providing discount properties to residential and commercial real estate investors.

MISSION

We source discounted, distressed properties for busy real estate investors so they can choose from a wider selection of deeply discounted deals.

OBJECTIVES

- First-year revenue $60,000
- Achieve profit before tax of $40,000 for the year ending 12/31/12
- Obtain relationships with three portfolio lenders with REO inventory
- End the year with a buyers list of 1,000 real estate investors

STRATEGIES

- Build our network and professional relationships within the investor community
- Cultivate relationships with REO agents
- Obtain access to nationwide MLS and database of cash buyers

PLANS

- Attend local REIA meeting each month beginning 1/1/12
- Buy a FreedomSoft license by 2/1/12
- Launch buyer and seller websites by 2/15/12
- Launch Facebook advertising campaign to build buyers list by 3/1/12
- Obtain a nationwide list of REO agents and asset managers by 2/15/12
- Contact a minimum of two potential investors per week beginning 1/1/12
- Contact a minimum of two REO agents/asset managers per week beginning 2/15/12

The vision is to grow their wholesaling business into a $500,000 annual revenue real estate company within the next three years that specializes in providing discount properties to residential and commercial real estate investors. The mission is to source discounted distressed properties for busy real estate investors so they can choose from a wider selection of deeply discounted deals. If you're at a real estate investor association (REIA) meeting and you're a wholesaler and you meet somebody and they ask, "What do you do?" drop that line on them. I bet you're going to get their business card.

The objectives are first-year revenue of sixty grand; achieve profit before tax of forty-thousand per year, ending on a specified date; obtain relationships with three portfolio lenders; and end the year with a buyers list of a thousand real estate investors. The strategies are what they know they need to do in order to make this work, and the plan consists of the tasks they're going to do to achieve the strategies. That's the whole business plan on one page. Isn't that a lot easier than trying to figure out a fifty- or sixty- page document? There is a time and a place to crank out the fifty- or sixty-page thing; but right now you just want to be clear about your private money program and you want to be able to articulate that program to those potential partners.

Your Value Statement – The Elevator Speech

Your value statement is an awesome answer to the question "What do you do?" It's also known as your elevator speech because if you ride an elevator with someone and they ask you what you do, they should have a very clear idea by the time you reach their floor. The framework for it is "I _____ so that _____ ." For example, "I *put together lucrative real estate investments* so that *my investment partners will make safe, consistent profits.*" The goal is to get a response of "Cool!" instead of "Oh, that's nice" while they walk away. So try to make it just a little sexy.

Partner Vision; Periscope up!

Once you have created and can articulate your value statement, you can then practice what I call "partner vision." Partner vision is a new way of assessing people you meet in your everyday life as potential investment partners. It's like radar: ping, ping, ping, potential partner, ping, ping, ping, potential partner. Be ever-vigilant in your search for potential investment partners because that's how you create and control the funding for your deals. I know I'm not schlepping down to Bank of America or begging some mortgage broker to underwrite my loan, wasting my time for two months just to have them tell me no at the last minute. I don't play that game and neither do you as of today.

Investment Criteria; That's How We Do It

Your investment criteria are what you're investing in and how you're going to make money. These are the specific types of properties you're looking for. Your criteria are what to articulate clearly to your acquisitions team, your realtor if you're working with a buyer's agent, or a bank if you're working with one to get packages of foreclosed properties. People with properties want to know what you want to acquire. You never want to be the guy who says, "Oh, I don't know. What have you got?" Eew! Don't be that person. I want you be crystal clear on your investment criteria and your ability to communicate those criteria to anybody, at any time. That is crucial if you want to stay focused and successfully raise private money before you have a deal.

Money First or Deal First; The Chicken or the Egg?

I get this question all the time: "Susan, do I go out and get a deal under contract and then look for private money, or do I first look for private money and then go and find a deal?" My preference is to get the money first and then go looking for the deal. Why? It keeps you out of desperation mode. Once you get a deal under contract, the clock is ticking. You don't want every person you approach to see a wild look in your eye that says, "Oh, no! I need some money; I need some money." People see that look and they're repelled by it. On the other hand, if you raise the cash before you need it, you're a cash buyer. Cash buyers get the deeper discounts; cash buyers get awarded the deals before anybody else because they can close quicker; cash buyers are in control because they have the cash. The reason most people don't do it is because they can't clearly articulate to their investors exactly what it is they're going to be buying.

If you go to an investor and they ask, "What are you going to be investing in?" and you answer, "Oh… well… we're looking at some duplexes and also we heard that Indiana might be good and…" – that's not going to work. But if you say, "We're looking for single-family homes in these particular five zip codes for which the purchase price is below sixty percent of the market value and the repaired value is no more than seventy-five percent of market value. We're going to hold for five years, and we have an anticipated profit of $14,000 per house" – now you're talking! Do you see how much easier it is to have that conversation with your investor and successfully raise money before you even have a house under contract? That's why it is so important to have specific investment criteria. It's the key to raising money before you need it, and to having money on hand when you need it.

Your Investment Criteria; Take It or Leave It

I am asked all the time to partner in deals, but my criteria are very specific. For me to consider a deal it must have a $5-million- plus purchase price, no capital improvements or extensive rehab, and the investment partners must already be lined up so I don't have to raise private money for the deal. If it meets those criteria, I have them input the deal into ianalyzerei.com and send me the complete twenty-six-page report that it creates along with personal financial statements for all the partners. If I like what I see, I'll call them. That's pretty specific, isn't it?

I ask them to input the whole deal into something that gives me a full report so that the initial work is in their court. Why should I spend hours analyzing deals that I'm never going to do? I have no desire to spend my time that way. That is the attitude that your potential private money partners are going to have, too. And that's why it's essential that you be able to articulate clearly exactly what it is that you are doing.

Chapter Three

UNMASKING YOUR SECRET IDENTITY

*"Now, I'm not saying I'm Wonder Woman.
I'm just saying no one has ever seen me and
Wonder Woman in the same room."*

−Wonder Woman

Credibility; Inspiring Trust

Personal credibility is a funny thing. There are some people you entrust with your life the minute you meet them. There are others you "don't trust as far as you could throw them" (as my grandmother would say). Why is that? What builds the personal credibility that some people just seem to have naturally even if they've never accomplished a single, notable thing? What is it they do differently?

Self-Respect, Margaritas, and Flip-Flops

Personal credibility is dependent upon the ability to inspire trust and respect in others. To inspire trust and respect in others, you have to first respect yourself. If you want people to respect your investment opportunities, you have to first respect your investment opportunities, and your investors' time, energy, and money. When others believe, trust, and have and confidence in you, then you have their respect.

When you have the respect of others, your self-worth and your confidence increases – there's no way it can't, and it feels really good. When you receive respect, you're more self-accepting. I do speaking engagements all over the country in front of hundreds of people. I am a respected investor, educator, and author. And yet here I am, maybe sixty to sixty-five pounds overweight, and wearing flip-flops for goodness sake. Respect is not image-conscious.

When I used to meet with my private money partners, I would meet with them in flip-flops and cargo shorts at a Mexican restaurant in Denver called La Loma for giant margaritas, chips, and salsa. That's just me. Not long ago I was speaking at a conference, and while we were setting up I was in the back chatting with Mira, my audio-visual guy. Now, I know my stuff, but I told him I was a little nervous because it was going to be the most-well-attended event I had ever done. I said, "I know they're coming here to hear me, and I want to give them a great experience and I want to give them really great knowledge and the plan they need to go out and do what they need to do. But I'm nervous." Mira just looked at me and said, "You know what? Just be you, and you'll be fine. You're the flip-flops and margarita girl! Who doesn't love that?" The point is that no matter how accomplished you are, no matter how respected you are, you're always going to have those moments of self-doubt. The challenge is to do what you can every day to overcome them, and go on in spite of them.

The Authentic You

The more respect and trust you can inspire in others, the more those self-doubts will just fall away. You might not believe this yet, but maybe you'll remember it in five or six years and you'll know I was right. The credibility problem that you likely have has nothing to do with anyone else. It's all you. I went through the same thing. What I know now is that even though I am overweight and obsessively comfortable in flip-flops, I know that my value isn't contingent on those things. How you view your credibility is huge, especially in your investor relations division. When you're self-accepting, it increases your authenticity. I'm the flip-flops and margarita girl, and that's authentic. If I started walking around wearing pantyhose and Spanx® and a dress and wobbling on high heels, people would look at me sideways saying, "What the heck?" That's not the authentic me.

When you are authentic, others instinctively believe and trust in you. I was pitching to the same people in Denver whom other people were pitching to, so why was I successful in raising private money when they weren't? They were wearing suits, and I was wearing shorts. They were holding their meetings in fancy rented offices and pretending the offices were theirs. Those guys were not authentic. I just said, "Let's go to La Loma and get a giant fish-bowl margarita." You can don your Armani® suit, and sport a Rolex®, and cruise up in your fancy rented sports car, and rent your fancy penthouse office, but people will see through it. Put your feet in the other guy's shoes. As an investor, would you want to hand some slickster $100,000 or would you invest with someone who knows who they are, what they're doing, and where they're going? I think that's why I was so successful doing this. It's just about being you.

Seven Steps to Inspire Credibility

There are seven steps to inspire credibility. First of all you have to know your stuff. If I had been sitting across from any of my investment partners in that Mexican restaurant with a margarita in my hand oohing and ahing about what I was investing in, do you think I would have landed a single deal or connected with a single investor? Flip-flops or not, I would have been turned down flat. You have to know your stuff.

Second, you have to keep your commitments, both big and small. If I tell someone I will meet them at La Loma at 2:00 o'clock, I do not walk in at 2:01, because I would be breaking a commitment to that person. Whether it's about a million-dollar deal or a minute late, a commitment is a commitment. If you break the small ones, people will expect that you'll break the big ones, too.

The third and fourth steps go hand in hand: Honor confidences and avoid gossip. The brand you will be creating for yourself is one of transparency, but not everyone presents that way. Respect that. If someone tells you something in private, keep it private. Real estate investing communities in every city across the nation are small. We all know each other and we all know what's going on. We know who's doing well, who's not doing well, who's flaking out, and who's not flaking out. We also know who can keep confidences and who can't be trusted to keep things on the down-low. Don't gossip about people; it breaks trust. Trust is your greatest asset.

Five, don't ever tear someone else down in an effort to make you look better. That always backfires. It shows your insecurities and damages your professionalism. They do what they do. You do what you do. Leave it at that.

Six, know yourself — the good, bad, and ugly. Be transparent. That's why I like Facebook so much. I get to see the transparent people. I get to see pictures of their dogs, pictures of them camping, where they're going on vacation, and so many other aspects of their real lives. It makes them real and genuine. People trust that.

The seventh step is choose to value others. Don't just blow someone off; engage yourself with the person in front of you.

Ask more and listen the most. Create credible interactions. When you're standing there talking to somebody and all of a sudden you look over their shoulder or at your watch, what does that do to the dynamic? It's hard to build credible interactions with someone when you show you are disinterested in them. Nothing breaks a connection faster than when you feel like the person you're speaking with is wasting their time. It's the same when somebody comes up to you at a party and shakes your hand but then immediately they're looking for the next best person to go and talk to. It's insincere. Don't be that person.

Finding Your Lost Credibility

What happens when you lose credibility? Can you get it back? When the real estate market crashed back in 2008, it took a lot of good people down. I worked with a guy named Naveen who ran into this problem. Naveen is a cool guy who owned 150 units that he had financed with private money from friends and family. When the market crashed, he didn't have the cash flow to pay these people back. At first he tried to hide from it and not even acknowledge it was happening. He took the ostrich approach by sticking his head in the sand and hoping it would all just go away. When he came to me he was in a bad place. I told him, "We need to fix this. It's about being upfront and honest and acknowledging objectively what has gone on, and then fixing it. So we're going to reach out to every single investor, we're going to restructure the loans, you're going to start making payments, and you're going to make this right." Naveen was panicking. "Oh my goodness. They all want their money back. They're never going to go for this."

I took Naveen through a process I called "project reframe" to get him to reframe his whole opinion of himself. The first thing I had him do was to put together a spreadsheet of all the private money partners he had, listing how much they loaned him. Then I had him list how much interest he had already paid them.

He called me and said, "I can't believe these people. I'm looking at the spreadsheet. Don't these people know how much money they've made with me?" I laughed and said, "Exactly! So when you have the conversations with these investors, ask them where else they could have made that kind of return in that horrible of a market." Then he marched back out with that frame of mind and restructured every single deal. Everybody was happy. The moral of the story is this: If you have a credibility problem, it is often just your perceived credibility problem, and you're perpetuating it; no one else. If you're struggling with that, try to do one of your own project reframes. Acknowledge why you're feeling that way and see what you can do to change it. Credibility isn't about power, position, or experience; it's about inspiring trust and being the authentic you every single day.

Your Brand; Who Are You Again?

You might be thinking, "My company's just tiny. It's just me. I don't need a brand. Branding is for the big guys." Okay, then what makes you stand out? People who are selling undervalued houses have a lot of potential buyers to deal with, especially those dealing in foreclosure and pre-foreclosure properties. What makes you stand out? Why would they want to do business with you over anybody else? What makes you remarkable? What makes you different?

Remember Kiss? Here's a rock band that's been around since 1973. They started in New York – just some teenagers playing in their garage. They landed a couple of gigs, but they weren't going anywhere until Gene Simmons came up with a unique branding idea and Kiss was born. The Kiss brand is one of the most lucrative, lasting brands in the recording business today.

Another example is a girl named Stefani Germanotta, a singer/song-writer from New York. She released an album in 2006 called *Red* and *Blue* that received, at best, moderate success. When she figured out the power of branding in 2008, Lady Gaga was born. Since her rebrand, she has been selected as the icon of the decade and Time Magazine's second-most-influential person. She has thirty-seven million Twitter followers, has sold twenty-three million albums and sixty-five million singles, has five Grammys and thirteen MTV Video Music Awards. Stefani Germanotta didn't have a chance in hell of accomplishing that. Love her or hate her, she's a polarizing figure, and it's her brand that made her stand out.

It Takes Guts to Wear a Meat Dress

So what makes your brand distinct? What makes you memorable? What comes up when somebody Googles you? Rest assured you will be Googled. Have content online that impresses potential partners and clients. What about this social media thing? Maybe you know you should be on Twitter and LinkedIn and Facebook and all that stuff for your business, but you have absolutely no clue how to do it. It's about branding and how you present yourself online. It's about your web presence.

Here's the problem that most people have with branding: It took guts to dress up like Kiss. Can you imagine the first time those guys got all dressed up in their giant shoes, tights, and outrageous makeup and walked out on stage? How about the first time Lady Gaga decided to wear a meat dress on the red carpet? That takes guts. You have to put yourself out there and showcase what you offer. It feels like you're bragging, but if you don't make people aware of your accomplishments and talents, nobody else will.

Your Website

If you're just starting out, you're probably thinking, "Well, Susan, I'm not going to do a website because I don't have pictures and stuff to put on my website." You don't need any to start. That will happen. Get your site up and running. Get social. Share your successes and your challenges on Twitter and Facebook. Give recommendations on LinkedIn. Give compliments and be transparent. People love compliments. Don't you love to be complimented? When you post something on Facebook and somebody likes it, don't you smile and think, "Ooh, they like it!" It's kind of cool that somebody else likes what you like, too. And it's nice when they validate you that way. So if wearing a meat dress is part of your branding strategy, be sure to take a picture of it and post it on Facebook so people can see it.

You are the one who has to drive your brand, and the best way to do it is to use your website to showcase your deals. Humans are visual creatures, especially men. If you're working with male investors, you have to show them visually so it resonates. Post pictures of properties you have invested in and outline details of your successes. Most important, post testimonials from anybody you can. Get testimonials from sellers, buyers, private lenders, bankers, tenants, and the guy at Home Depot where you get your lumber. Get them from anybody you come into contact with in your business. You should be asking them to provide a testimonial or some little blurb about how it was to work with you so you can share it with others. What, still no website? You need a website because people are going to want to know more about you and what you do. When you start making offers to your potential private money partners, they're going to go right home, they're going to put you in Google, and they're going to see what's there. They're going to type in your name and things like "ripoff," "scam," "review," "complaints," and "real estate" just to see what's out there. Control that messaging, and control what's out there about you.

Society's Tick: Social Proof

A societal tick that's becoming more prevalent these days is something called social proof. Social proof means I won't buy into your product or idea unless there is already a following. Nobody wants to do business with somebody that nobody else is doing business with. Most people don't want to be the first one at the party. I bet you're the same. If the party starts at 8:00, you'll get there at 8:10. If yours is the first car there, do you drive around the neighborhood a bit? I bet you do. I know I do. I drive around the block a few times. I have this one friend who throws parties all the time, and if I get over there too early, I know that there's a PetSmart™ right across the way and I can just go over and stock up on dog food and dog treats. If I come back and there are a couple of people there, then I don't feel as weird. It's important to have testimonials and examples to show that there are already lots of guests at your party.

Testimonials; Deposit Your Two Cents Here

Testimonials are also important because nobody really believes what we say about ourselves, but they'll usually believe an objective third party. That's why testimonials are so big in establishing the concept of social proof. I can tell you, "My Getting the Money coaching program is the best resource for real estate investors who want to achieve success fast." Your first thought is likely, "Well of course she's going to say that; she's promoting her coaching." So instead of that, I get testimonials from my coaching clients. I also have a Facebook business page where people can leave reviews. When I conduct a teleseminar or webinar, I always ask people to go to my Facebook business page and leave a comment. It's all about social proof! If you are working with a vendor, buyer, seller, tenant, or private money partner, tell them you value their feedback and ask them to go to your Facebook business page and leave a little blurb about what it was like to work with you. People are always happy to give you their two cents. When they do, boom! There it is on your Facebook page – positive testimonial content.

Social Media; "Oh, That Stuff"

If you're familiar with internet searches, you might be wondering, "How am I going to get my website to rank high in the search engines?" Who cares where your website ranks, because guess what comes up first? That's right – Facebook. Let Facebook do all the heavy lifting. All you have to do is plug in to their SEO engine to get ranked high in the search engines. That's why you need to be on LinkedIn; that's why you need to be on Twitter; and that's why you need to be on Facebook. They all provide you with great exposure.

I'm a bit of a Facebook stalker in that I like to keep tabs on the people I work with and the people I teach to see how they're doing. This guy I helped, Steven Scott, posted a picture of an apartment building he acquired (his first commercial property), and people were liking it and offering their congratulations. I typed in a "congrats" message, too, and then out of nowhere he posted, "Susan, thank you for all your hard work. If anybody wants to learn commercial real estate, buy Susan Lassiter-Lyons's books and materials. She's the best." It's amazing what can happen when you reveal your secret identity!

Chapter Four

CREATING YOUR PROGRAM; "IT LIVES! IT LIVES!"

"A successful man is one who can lay a firm foundation with the bricks others have thrown at him."

−David Brinkley

By now you should have figured out − and written down − your investment company's goals and overall mission statement. You should have a pretty clear idea of what you want your company to do. Now it's time to dig a little deeper into your investor relations division where I'll help you create your own specific but flexible private money program.

When someone asks you how much you need, you never want to say, "I don't know. What were you thinking?" That's a recipe for disaster. You don't want your prospect to control the conversation and feel like they have some control of the transaction, because they really don't. This program is yours. Because you know your specific investment criteria, you will know going into any of these conversations exactly how much you can afford to pay for the deals.

Debt Investors

The difference between a debt *investor* and an *equity* investor is that a debt investor makes the loan for a set payment and does not get to participate in the profits, whereas an equity investor provides capital in exchange for a share of the profits, cash flow, or equity. Here are some examples of how this works. First is a debt-investor example: Let's say that you're buying a four-unit apartment building for $350,000. You're getting seller financing for $250,000 and you're getting a private money loan from your Aunt Sally for $100,000. Seller financing means the seller of the property provides financing for you to buy their property, with the agreement you will be paying back the loan in installments plus interest. In this debt-investor example, you keep 100 percent ownership. The net profits for that four-unit apartment building go into your pocket. Aunt Sally gets an 8 percent return on her money (just simple interest) over a five-year term while you make monthly interest payments to her. You also make the installment payments to the seller. That's a simple debt example.

Equity Investors

Here is an equity-investor example: You are, again, buying this four-unit apartment building for $350,000, with seller financing of $250,000 and a private money loan from good ol' Aunt Sally, but this time Sally says, "I think I want a bigger piece." Now you decide to do it for a fifty-fifty split. So what you do is either form a limited liability company (LLC) with Aunt Sally and split the profits, or you can write Aunt Sally into the operating agreement for your existing LLC for that specific property and split the profits that way. If for some reason you don't make any money with the building in the first six months, Sally doesn't get any money. If your deal makes $1,000 each month, then she gets her $500 each month just like you.

Hybrid Deals

Here's a hybrid example. It's the kind of deal I like to do. It's a debt and equity hybrid. When I put these deals together I call them "debt investments with an equity kicker," meaning your investment partner is a debt investor, but you're going to give them a little something on the equity side if things go well – like a little surprise. So for the $350,000 four-unit apartment building, you get a private money loan from Aunt Sally for $360,500. Why did she loan more than the purchase price? She loaned the extra $10,500 because you're charging a 3 percent acquisition fee up front for putting this deal together. You're making three points cash right at the closing table, and Aunt Sally gets to make money on both ends. It's a 75/25 split ownership with Sally. You will pay her 5 percent quarterly in simple interest as a debt investor, and a 25 percent ownership split as an equity investor. If that property makes $1,000 profit every month after you make Sally's loan payment, you get $750 and Sally gets $250. Kind of cool, huh?

Sticking to Your Investment Criteria

You can structure your deals any way you want, but be very specific about what you're investing in. Instead of just saying, "I invest in apartment buildings," be as specific as "I invest in twenty- to fifty-unit apartment buildings, Class C, in the County of Denver, Colorado, between $30,000 and $40,000 per door." Boom. That is what you invest in. And when you tell your investor that is what you're investing in, and they agree to fund it, but instead you get an office building – that's no good. "No bueno!" as we like to say. Your deals have to match your specific criteria and what you are disclosing to your potential private money partner.

How Much Should I Pay My Investors?

At this point you may be wondering, "How much should I pay my investors?" So my question back to you is, "How much can you afford to pay your investors?" I can't give you a definitive answer because I have no context for the deal you're doing. It's the same as asking me, "Susan, what kind of car should I buy?" I don't know. Do you like four-wheel-drives or convertibles? Who knows? There has to be some context to that conversation.

What you can afford to pay is based on different variables. How much are you raising? What is the cash flow of your property? What is the equity of the property? What is the debt coverage ratio? *Debt coverage ratio means* "Can the cash flow from this property actually pay the monthly mortgage payment and still have enough profit left over for me?" That's important if you're working with a debt partner.

What is the rate of return you can afford to pay? You find these answers by doing the math. So strap in because it's time to do some basic math.

Annual Cash Flow

To figure out the annual cash flow, look at the gross annual income and subtract the annual operating expenses, the annual loan payments, and the annual income taxes. The annual cash flow is different from the net operating income, or NOI, because it takes the debt service into account. Debt service is just a fancy way of saying mortgage payment. Your offer should usually contain some contingencies like a loan approval contingency, clean and clear title, review of the seller's books, review of all lease agreements, and a property inspection (your escape clause in case something isn't working out).

Rental Income and Expenses

In order to determine the rental income and expenses, get a copy of the *rent roll* and copies of all current leases from the seller. The rent roll is just a list of all the tenants, their unit numbers, how much rent they pay each month, and the terms of their leases. When you look at the rent roll and the leases and how they relate to the number of units in the property, you're going to come up with what's known as a *vacancy rate*. Vacancy rate means how many units are vacant, and is expressed in a percentage. A 4.1 percent vacancy rate means that you expect it to be vacant one month every two years, or one divided by 24. The vacancy rate can be the actual rate, or it can be *pro forma*, which means what you think the rate will normally be even if right now it's 100 percent occupied.

Property Costs

You're going to need to know the cost of the property, the property type, the fair market value for that property, and the appreciation rate. Those are things any realtor can tell you. The appreciation rate for commercial properties (*commercial* means five units or more) is solely based on an increase in cash flow, because commercial properties aren't affected that much by what's happening in the market around them. Their value is determined almost exclusively by their own cash flow. Don't forget to factor in the selling expenses!

The Interest Rate

For financing, you're going to need to figure out what kind of rate this deal supports. Can it support only 4 percent or could you go as high as 7 percent? Can you factor in some points or afford to pay more to the lender? What fees, if any, can you afford to pay from this deal? To put this in perspective, your calculations can change depending on whether you're going to use an existing private lender or a family member. Private lenders have been around the block, so you're going to have to pay points, fees, and likely a higher-than-normal interest rate.

Screeners; Your Deal Filter

I normally do some initial figuring that I call "screeners" to help me decide if the deal warrants a closer look. First I like to calculate the net operating income, the debt coverage ratio, and the cap rate. The net operating income is the gross income minus vacancies and expenses. The debt coverage ratio is the net operating income divided by the annual debt payments or mortgage payments. What lenders usually like to look for in terms of a debt coverage ratio is 1.2 or 1.3. All that means is once you pay all the mortgage payments for the year, your operating income remains 20 percent (1.2) to 30 percent (1.3) above even. The cap rate is the net operating income divided by the fair market value or, expressed another way, the NOI divided by the cap rate. You can usually get cap rates online by market or from a realtor. They are normally calculated for multiple-unit properties, not for single-family dwellings.

So let's see how this works. *Cash-on-cash return* is the cash flow of your investment divided by the amount you've invested. If you wanted to calculate the annual cash dividend that a property is throwing off to a potential investor, here's how that would look: Let's say the net cash flow (or the return on debt service plus fees) is $25,000 and your private money partner is willing to invest $125,000. Divide $25,000 by $125,000 and you get 0.2. Multiply by 100 to get the percentage. In this case, your cash-on-cash return is 20 percent.

That's a quick and dirty way to see a basic return on your deal. But if you want to take other factors into account, such as the loan payment or property appreciation, calculate the *internal rate of return* (or yield). Let's say you have a $300,000 note for a twelve- month term, with an interest rate of 10 percent, and your lender is charging two points. Then it's $300,000 divided by 10 percent to get the annual mortgage payment of $30,000. Two points equal

$6,000. So $36,000 divided by $300,000 is a yield of 12 percent to your investor. The interest in this example is simple interest. If you wanted to amortize your debt payments to your investors, you can get a simple amortization schedule online or pick up a mortgage calculator that will calculate it for you. The internal rate of return is a calculation I use to make the point to my short-term lenders that they need to go long term because they can make long-term rates with half the headaches.

"Excuse Me, Do You Have the Timing?"

We're still trying to solve the question, "How much should I pay my investors?" You need to know the *timeframe* – a short-term investment or long-term investment – and the *payment schedule*. You can make the rate anything – 2 percent, 10 percent, 18 percent – just be sure you're not charging too much or paying too much. Follow the usury laws in your area.

For the timeframe, determine how long you need the money. Is this a rehab that you can flip and be out of in six months? Maybe you build in a buffer and call it eight months. Maybe you build in a big buffer and call it twelve months. And if it pays off early, there's no prepayment penalty.

For the payment schedule, determine how often you're going to be paying your investors. You can pay them monthly, quarterly, or annually, or you can make deferred payments until the deal flips.

Or you can offer a dividend reinvestment opportunity; here your investors don't get a payout at all. They elect instead to have their dividends reinvested right back into the fund. You can structure your deal in many different ways.

Residential Buy and Hold; Both Perspectives

Let's put this to the test. Let's say you have a residential buy and hold for which the purchase price is $137,900, and it needs $22,000 in repairs. When it's all fixed up it's going to be worth $213,000. You have two debt partners who are going to do the deal. You're going to pay one of them 5.5 percent and the other one 6.5 percent. The loan is on a five-year term and the rent on the house is $1,200 a month. Analyze this property two ways: one from your perspective to see how much you're going to make on the deal, and another from your private money partners' perspective to see what they're going to make on the deal.

Here is an analysis from your perspective: The potential rental income for year one is $14,400 less vacancy, $720 in credit loss, and $2,880 in operating expenses. So your net operating income is going to be $10,800. Subtract the annual debt service (the total mortgage payment that you're going to pay out to your two debt investors) of $11,511. So you're losing $711 each year before taxes. Not so great. In year two, you will lose $495; in year three $275; in year four $50. In year five, my goodness, you made a whopping $179 for the whole year. Sweet! Is this a deal you would be interested in doing? Not likely!

Now let's look at the deal from your debt investment partners' perspective. Debt Partner One invests $79,900, and you're paying him 5.5 percent. His monthly payment is $454, and his total return over the five-year term is $27,240. His cash-on-cash return is 34 percent. It's a great deal from his perspective. Debt Partner Two is getting an even higher point value, and his cash-on-cash is 38 percent.

I do this to illustrate a point because I see it happen all the time. You get these investment partners, and you're so freaking excited that somebody finally wants to invest with you that you run out and snag the next deal that comes down the pike. Then you find yourself in trouble by investing in a bad deal because you focused on what your private money partner can make, but you neglected to see how you're getting screwed. It's not worth doing a deal if you're only going to make $179 in five years! Even if the property appreciates in that time, appreciation doesn't pay the bills.

Residential Fix and Flip; Both Perspectives

Let's look at a residential fix and flip example. The purchase price is $67,900, and repairs will cost you $43,000. Your as-repaired- value (ARV) will be $148,000. You have one equity partner on a six-month term, and the price when you flip it is going to be $144,000. Here's what it looks like from your perspective: The selling expenses are going to be $8,880, and the cumulative rehab and holding expenses are going to be

$945. Don't forget that, rehabbers. You will need to pay the light bill, the water bill, and all that stuff. Initial purchase price: $113,400.

Profit / Loss	Month 1	Month 2	Month 3	Month 4	Month 5
Projected After-Repair Sale Value	$ 148,000	$ 148,000	$ 148,000	$ 148,000	$ 148,000
FMV Adjustment Option (+/-)	-	-	-	-	-
Adj Projected After-Repair Sale Value	$ 148,000	$ 148,000	$ 148,000	$ 148,000	$ 148,000
Selling Expenses	(8,880)	(8,880)	(8,880)	(8,880)	(8,880)
Cumulative Rehab & Holding Expenses	(945)	(1,890)	(2,835)	(3,780)	(4,725)
Initial Purchase Price	$ (113,400)	$ (113,400)	$ (113,400)	$ (113,400)	$ (113,400)
Total Profit (Loss) if Sold by Month End	$ 24,775	$ 23,830	$ 22,885	$ 21,940	$ 20,995

If you sell by the end of month one, the profit is $24,775. If you hang on until month two, it goes down to $23,830. If you sell it in month three, it's $22,885. In month four, $21,940. In month five, $20,995. So if it takes you five months to sell the thing, you're making about $21,000. Is it worth doing? I think that's worth doing!

Cool. So you're in. Let's take a look and see what happens to your equity partner, Jim Smith. You have a partner profit share, so your projected cash (before tax) if you sell in month one is $24,775. The managing partner's (that's you) profit share is $12,388, and Jim Smith's share of the profit is $12,388. If it takes you six months to sell, he gets $10,025.

Let's see about his cash-on-cash return. If you sell it in month one, his cash-on-cash return is 10.9 percent. Not bad. The worst-case scenario: if it takes you six months, his cash-on-cash return goes down to 8.8 percent. Could you sell that to an equity partner? It's a better return than the banks would give him, so the point I really want to drive home to you is that just because a deal is great for your investment partner doesn't mean it's a slam-dunk for you, and vice-versa. You have to run it from both perspectives for the deal to make sense.

What Is Good for Your Investment Partner?

I've learned it's very helpful to find out what your investment partner's money is currently earning. I'll ask them, "So what is the money that you're considering investing in my deal earning right now?" Often you will hear that people are losing money or that they are making maybe 3 or 4 percent. Your next comment should be something like, "Really? You're only making 2 percent on that? Well, what if I could double it?" That's a major win-win because you're doubling the return that they are currently getting, which makes them happy, and you're only paying 4 percent, which makes you happy. Obviously you're not going to say that if somebody's making 10 percent on their money, but for those making peanuts on their savings and investments, a conversation like that might be in both of your interests. Find out what they're making and how you can improve on it.

How long will their money be earning? You can have separate rates for short-term, mid-term, and long-term investors. You can structure it any way you want. If you want somebody to commit their money long term, give them a reward for that. Real estate lenders are always going to want a higher rate of return than friends and family. That's a fact. Think about paying a bonus in points, like a quarter point or half point on each deal you do if they commit their funding to you for long-term, multiple deals.

Here is what I did with Rick, who was my very first private money partner: Once I got his $300,000, I didn't want to lose it. So I said, "If you commit this money to me for the next twelve months, so I have exclusive use; and if you say no to anybody else who wants you to invest; I'll give you an extra half point cash on every single deal we do." Rick was down with that, and so were my other partners. Every penny of their investment money was then mine to grow.

Disclosure; What You Say Is What You Do

I keep bringing up the point that you can structure the deal however you want — what you pay, how you pay, when you pay. In this business it's all about disclosure. Whatever you tell them it's going to be, that's what it is. You can pay your investor monthly, quarterly, or annually. You can even tell them, "Because these are short-term loans and they're flips, we'll let the interest accrue for the six months. I'll just pay you off after the flip when we sell the property." You can make it anything you want as long as you disclose it and as long as that's cool with your investor.

The Extension Clause; Your Safety Net

What happens when your short-term investment turns into a long- term marathon? There are lots of reasons for this: your flip doesn't flip; market conditions do crazy things; you have a fire. How do you think the conversation with your investor might go if you knew there was no way the deal would close by the term date? "I know I was supposed to pay you back in six months but the project's taken us longer than we thought. We're going to need another two months. Is that okay?" The answer: "No, that's not okay. I want my money back now according to the term we set." Now you're in deep doo-doo.

The best thing to do is plan for this in advance with something called an extension clause. Write a contingency in the promissory note as the deal is being forged in case stuff happens. Say to your debt investor, "This is a six-month term, but just in case we go over, let's plan for automatic extensions. If I don't pay it back by the six months, let's say that my 4 percent interest rate will jump to 6 percent every month I am over the six-month term. We can cap it there until the note is paid in full. What do you say?" I've had that exact conversation with investors and they've remarked to me, "Yay! I sure hope your project gets blown so I can make more money." I laughed, but thought how they'd be whistling a completely different tune if there was no extension clause and I couldn't pay them back by term end. Have these conversations up front and plan for the imperfect.

By now you've figured out what business you're in and have had time to think about your business plan, business objectives, and goals. Now drill down and say, "Knowing all of this and knowing how to be very clear on my investment criteria, how do I craft my private money program?" Based on your investment criteria, figure out deal by deal what you can afford to pay. Know what you can pay your investment partners, what you can pay a debt investor, what you can pay an equity investor, and what you can offer a hybrid investor. Calculate your return on the investment and their return on the investment. That will answer the question "What do I pay my investors?"

Chapter Five

BUILDING YOUR TEAM

"Coming together is a beginning. Keeping together is progress. Working together is success."

–Henry Ford

Yes, You Need a Team

We're going to talk about teams because nobody can do this alone. Going back to the "Your Investment Divisions" chart, we're now going to focus on the areas below your buy-and-hold, fix- and-flip, and wholesaling divisions. Here you'll find acquisitions, sales, construction, and property management. That's just the tip of the iceberg.

I know there are a lot of people who want to run a one-man or one-woman show. I did, too – for far too long, until I finally learned that you don't hire for where you are now; you hire for where you want to be. I am not a one-woman show; I have a great team backing me up. They are the reason my company has experienced explosive revenue growth over the last four years.

With thirty prospects, your goal is one to ten lender partners for a marketing process you only have to do once. The number one mistake I've seen people make is to try to do this all alone with no team. Trying to fill all four divisions yourself by acting as your own general contractor is ridiculous. On top of that, someone still has to manage the properties and do all the other tasks associated with making this business and all of its divisions run. You need a team.

I like to *partner with strength*. That means I align myself with people with the highest levels of expertise. The best partner for you is not somebody just like you. A good business partner or team member possesses strength in your area of weakness. Look for people who complement you and add to what you're doing, not take away from it.

Your In-House Team

There are two elements of teams: your *in-house team* and your *supporting team*. First up in your in-house team is *acquisitions*. Once you develop your very specific deal criteria and your marketing channels, consider hiring an *acquisitions manager*. He or she will help you market in each of the deal-flow channels, because you're doing lots of different marketing to bring in deals (or you should be). Your acquisitions manager works with real estate agents, wholesalers, and REO agents. They contact the banks directly from inventory and coordinate with buyers' agents. If you are offered a deal as part of your lead flow campaign, but it's not right for you, your acquisitions manager can pass it along to your wholesaling division. There's money in those leads – even in the deals you don't do. This person can be contract/hourly or a straight commission salesperson.

Consider also hiring a *sales manager* to manage your fix-and-flip and wholesaling divisions. They'd be in charge of building those buyers lists and developing relationships with wholesalers and buyer's agents. This person can be a real estate agent if you want to work closely with a real estate agent.

You should consider a construction manager for your fix-and-flip division. This person would be a general contractor who manages all aspects of what's going on in your fix-and-flip business. The worst part about rehabbing is having to find a new construction team for every project. For this business, a good general contractor is pure gold. Once you have one, you never have to hunt for another, and you don't have the headache of dealing with subcontractors because it's all outsourced for a great price.

For your buy-and-hold division, a property manager is a must. You might think you don't need one when you have a limited number of units, but when I had only two units, I hired a property manager. Pay them a percentage of the rents collected, but don't ever pay them an incentive to sign new leases! I made that mistake once. I thought it was a great idea because they'd rent out all my vacant units and in turn I'd give them $50 cash for every new lease. But I ended up with a whole bunch of one-month leases with the deposits waived. My building filled up with vagrants, and after I had handed over the $50 per lease everyone moved out and the whole process started again. Be smart about these things.

Your Supporting Team

I base my buying decisions on value, so one of the most important members of my supporting team is my *appraiser*. I use the same appraiser on every single deal. A lot of people say, "Don't the banks order the appraisals?" But I don't deal with banks. I have my own private money. So I use my team and not some schmo that a bank tells me to use. My appraiser is very accurate. I provide him with my repair budget and an itemized list of what I was planning to do with the property, and he gives me the *after repair value* (ARV) and a *comparative market analysis*. This package is not cheap, but it gives me very accurate numbers with which to work. *Licensed residential appraisers* are authorized to assess properties up to $1 million in value, and *certified residential appraisers* can assess properties over $1 million in value. A *certified general appraiser* has the authorization to deal with both residential and commercial properties. Just make sure you pick the right one for what you're doing and for what fits your investment criteria.

Another member of your supporting cast is the *inspector*. The purpose of the inspection is to determine the condition of the major systems, identify safety issues, and determine the habitability of the home – not obvious cosmetic defects. So you don't necessarily need one for every property. It's your decision whether you need one for your business model. Just make sure the inspector doesn't waste time and money examining the hardwood floors when he should be assessing the rotting roof sheathing or the heating system.

It's important to work with a creative *title* company representative. Use one who specializes in working with real estate investors and investment properties. You will understand more about the title company rep when we go over closing the deal. There aren't a lot of title company representatives who will sit back and allow you to take control of all aspects of the closing, so you'll want to find one who understands what you're doing and how you're doing it. Find one who supports your way of doing business.

Realtors are the necessary evil of real estate investing. Real estate investors are always asking, "Why can't we just do it ourselves? Why do we have to pay them to do this for us?"

But the right realtor can be a major asset, whereas the wrong realtor can make your life hell and make you broke. You might work with one who tells you no a lot. "No, you can't do that." "No, I won't submit this." "No, that offer will never get accepted." "No, you can't do a loan because of the Safe Act." Here's the thing: Realtors are often under the mistaken impression that we work for them. They think they get to tell us what's what. Here's what I say: Realtors work for you. They make the offer you tell them to make. They write the contract you tell them to write. If they won't, then they don't get to work for you. Find a good one because they can be a great asset, and do not work with one who puts constraints on your business.

Your *insurance agent* is important to your business because you need appropriate insurance coverage. You should consider *errors and omissions* insurance, loss of rental *income coverage*, and special coverage for your vacant properties. There are very few hazard insurance providers that will cover vacant properties. Many investors find that out the hard way when there's vandalism or someone breaks into a vacant property and steals tools or kicks down new drywall. Make sure that you have the right kind of insurance for what you're doing.

You need a *bookkeeper*. Bookkeepers are cheap, and my bookkeeper does it all. She charges me maybe sixty-five dollars a month. Can you afford that much in order not to have to do it yourself? Yes, you can. Get a bookkeeper. Doing your own books is the worst use of your valuable time. I bought a copy of QuickBooks™ and installed it on my computer. My bookkeeper does my books in QuickBooks and sends me a local backup copy each month that I use to update my records. I think you can even automatically sync your records online. Don't do your own books.

A good chartered *public accountant* (CPA) is not just a numbers-cruncher. You can use them for tax preparation, business and personal financial planning, and to help you set up effective accounting systems. I now have a bookkeeper, a CPA, and a virtual CFO, and I don't have to involve myself in any of the low- level numbers tasks. It's not worth my time. I don't want to get pulled off task or, even worse, pulled away from my vacation to have to answer some ridiculous financial question that somebody else can find the answer to.

If you're in a state where you need a *closing attorney*, make sure the one you use is well-versed in titles, will protect you from fraudulent transactions, and will file your documents in a timely manner. They should also be available to review and draft documents and answer your questions for a reasonable amount or maybe even free.

I highly recommend a *landlord and tenant attorney*. If you're a buy-and-hold investor and you have tenants, this person helps a lot. You can let them deal with serving notices, evictions, and zoning violations that end up in court. It's best to outsource all that court time to an attorney.

You should also line up a *securities attorney*. If you're going to be raising private money and structuring your business to pool money as a syndicator, or if you're going to be a group sponsor doing bigger offers, you should consider using a securities attorney. The minute you start taking in funds from multiple investment partners and putting them into a common interest, it becomes a security. It's better to have your ducks lined up by an attorney than to be invited to a little "chat" with an agent from the Securities and Exchange Commission (SEC).

Portfolio lenders are small banks and credit unions local to your subject property. Because these smaller banks don't have to follow the rules, they tend to finance properties in their local communities. That's why they're also called *community banks*. I use portfolio lenders a great deal when I want to pay off my private lenders. I can use my private money partner's funds to acquire a property, fix up that property, and while I'm seasoning that property. Then I go to the portfolio lender for refinancing to pay off my private lender so I can start over with the lender's money on a different project.

Portfolio lenders do other cool things, too. I got an email a couple of months ago from somebody who wrote, "I bought your Portfolio Loan Blueprint, and it worked!" I find it funny how people seem genuinely shocked when my program works for them. Why would I sell something that doesn't work? That guy told me he had just gotten a $600,000 business line of credit from a portfolio lender for his real estate investing company.

Another super-cool thing they do is something called master loan commitments. The portfolio lender says, "We're willing to underwrite you once for a perpetual loan." So I give them my specific investment criteria and tell them something like, "I'm acquiring single family homes at X price point that will need X amount of fix up. The value's going to be X when I'm finished, and X is how I'm positioning them. I'm buying, holding, or flipping them." The bank will say, "Okay, that's the criteria; we get it. Now let's take a look at you. Submit your financials." They look at your tax returns, your pay stubs, the financial statement for your business, and any holdings you have. Often they will then come back with a term letter saying, "We agree to fund up to $5 million in purchases for the next twelve months as long as they all match the specific criteria you gave us and nothing in your financial position materially changes. Here's the rate. Here's the fee. It's approved." How awesome is that? Someone just handed you $5 million in financing to use anytime you want to!

Every great player has a coach. Your coach is your advisor, consultant, motivator, and biggest cheerleader. They also bring credibility and experience to what you're doing. I've always had a coach for whatever I did. When I started playing t-ball at eight years old, I had a coach. When I ran track, I had a track coach. When I played tennis, I had a tennis coach. When I decided to start my mortgage company, I sought out an expert in mortgage origination and developing the types of funds I was developing, and I hired him to be my coach. Now that I have a seven-figure business, I need a business coach to help me grow.

You need private *money partners or investors.* These relationships are the absolute key to a successful business, so treat them like gold because that's what they are. My first investment partner, Rick, is awesome. The only time I ever said no to Rick was when he asked me to fix him up with girls. "Sorry, Rick. That's not the kind of business I run. You'll have to talk to your dating coach about that one!" Because managing your investment partners is such an important piece of the puzzle, I've devoted the next chapter to nurturing those investor relationships.

Find a loan servicer. If you're doing private money loans, either as a borrower or a broker, you should not be servicing them yourself. By servicing I mean taking and processing the payments. If I were to send Rick (or any of my money partners) a mortgage payment, he'd fire back, "What do I do with this? Can't you just handle it for me?" So I set up accounts with a loan servicer, and when I pay her she sends my money partners their proceeds. She takes a very nominal fee but provides all the accounting my partners need and even has online access so they can check the status of my loans, see the payments, and see their cuts. A loan servicer adds an extra level of professionalism.

One of the biggest mistakes you can make when you get a private money partner is to assume they know how all this works. They don't. They're relying on you as an expert to walk them through it. Don't just leave them to their own devices. Set up something professional for them. Tell them, "Here's how this is going to work. The funds go into escrow at the loan servicing company. You can log in at any time to check the status of the loan. They're going to cut you the proceeds, so tell them how you want it – check or direct deposit." That's a higher level of professionalism and gives your partner a greater sense of security. No monkey business. Your private money partner will want to work with a professional, so make it as easy as possible for them rely on you and work with you.

Line up a self-directed IRA provider. The majority of your private money partners are going to be investing with their retirement money, so help facilitate the process of rolling over their 401k or their IRA to a self-directed IRA. If you just said, "Hey, Investor, you're going to need to get your IRA rolled over, so just go find a self-directed IRA provider and then call me back when the money is ready," how well do you think that would go over with your potential private money partner? Picture a lead balloon as your credibility: zero. Much better to say, "Let me conference you in on the phone with my contact at iDirect Law. They're going to take great care of you and walk you through this entire process. I'm going to be there every step of the way. The iDirect rep is also going to communicate with me about where you are in the process so I'll know how soon you'll be ready to invest with me."

You can use any provider you want, but I use New Direction Trust Company because they are good, and I get a referral fee every time I send one of my money partners to them. That's very cool because you need to monetize every single thing you can. Just make sure the provider you use offers true checkbook control. Circle it, underline it, highlight it, or do whatever is necessary to remember this, because you can get screwed here. True checkbook control means they're going to set your investor up with an LLC, a bank account, and a checkbook. Your money partner needs a physical checkbook. When you say, "The deal is closing on Friday, and I need you to cut a check to the title company for $187,000," your investor simply writes a check and sends it to the title company. They can also wire the funds from that LLC bank account. What you don't want is to lose a deal because your partner has to phone a custodian or administrator at A-1 Self-directed IRA Company and then fill out an online form and then figure out how to scan or fax it. Everything will be delayed by all the confusion. I've had money partners run into some serious delays and major headaches trying to handle it all themselves. And cheap self-directed IRA providers are no better.

When you find those relationships and companies that do what they say and not only serve you well, but your partners, too, it makes you look good. Looking good to your partners is a big part of being professional. Do you want to be a professional investor, or do you want to be just some schmo who plays with money?

Chapter Six

WHERE'S THE MONEY?

"Nothing will ever be attempted if all possible objections must first be overcome."

–Samuel Johnson

The Private Money Acceleration Plan; Bring Me a Bucket!

We've established that you need visibility, you need a plan, and you need to know what you want. Next you need to identify your private money prospects. Where are you going to find these people? Who are they, and where are they hiding? There are billions of dollars just waiting to come into your deals. You will find all of your private money prospects in three buckets. Bucket One is the friends-and-family bucket. Bucket Two is investors who are already actively investing in real estate. Bucket Three is people who are already making private loans for real estate.

I have put together what I call the Private Money Acceleration Plan, and it looks like this:

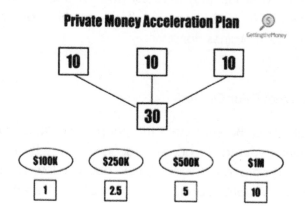

The tens in each square represent the three money-prospect buckets: friends and family, people investing in real estate, and people loaning money for real estate deals. Your plan can look a little different. You can have zero in one bucket and twenty in another bucket – however you want to mix and match and have potential partners in each. These are not people you're necessarily going to be partnering with, but people you want to present your opportunity to and see if there's some interest.

So ten, ten, and ten is going to give you thirty prospects – thirty people to talk to about your private money program and your real estate investment business. If you get one person to agree to work with you from those thirty people, you likely just got a minimum of $100,000 in private money. When I put this strategy in place, the real estate investors I was targeting had between $300,000 and $500,000 to invest. One hundred thousand is on the low side. If you get two at that level, and one with half of that, you'll have $250,000. If you get five out of the thirty to agree to work with you, you'll have a minimum of $500,000 in cash available to you. If you get ten people on board, or just one- third from your list who agree to work with you, that's *one million dollars* – minimum. Think about that if the first person you talk to says no. You have twenty-nine more people on your list. You don't just give up after having one conversation. At least I hope not. If you do, then you are not going to be in business long.

Bucket One: Dear Ol' Dad

Let's talk about Bucket One – the people who know you. It's your friends, your family, and your acquaintances. Bucket One is the easiest group to target with the absolute lowest lending rates available, but nobody ever wants to start there because of that secret identity issue. You think you have zero credibility with these people. Here's the good news: The people in Bucket One already know how real estate works. Most ordinary people already understand real estate and how people make money with it. According to Forbes, real estate is the number-three industry for creating billionaires, with a current total of 129 billionaires worldwide. The media is doing your job for you. The recovery is strong, real estate is coming back, and housing prices are starting to climb. The media is reporting on this and people see it. They've solved your whole "overcoming the objection to investing in real estate" problem already. You no longer have to have that discussion about how real estate makes money.

That's not the real issue, though, is it? The two big things that keep you from filling Bucket One are lack of experience, and you're afraid you are going to lose their money. It's not wrong to have a debilitating fear of losing your grandmother's retirement fund. That shows character and integrity. It's a huge responsibility, and one that you should take seriously. That's why you need to start running your business like a business, why you need to be crystal clear on your investment criteria, and why you need to know what you're doing. We talked about credibility, and the first of the seven steps to gain credibility is to *know your stuff.* If you know what you're doing, you will have the confidence to delight Grandma with safe, consistent returns on her retirement money.

We All Have a "Cousin Clay"

Remember the survey question "What is stopping you from going out and raising private money for your deals?" The number two answer was "I don't know anyone with any money."

Thinking that nobody you know has money is presumptuous. Let me tell you about my Cousin Clay. He is about four years older than I and he's one of my favorite cousins. Clay is a very talented musician, but all through high school he struggled with his weight, just like most of the people in my family. We have my grandfather to thank for that, I think, so we come by it honestly. He calls it the "Lassiter ass." Clay has it, too. In his senior year of high school, Clay's girlfriend Jeannie got pregnant, and as soon as they graduated they got married. About nine-and-a-half months later they had another baby, and another about three years after that. So here was my cousin, married with three kids before he even turned twenty-four. He started working as a cook, became a chef, and then went to work in a plant managing cooks who make those prepackaged soups and pies. He's worked there forever and plays in bands on the side. So Clay works at a factory that makes soups and pies, and his wife cleans houses, and they live in a plain-looking house in Kansas. Clay is the salt of the earth.

A couple of years ago his mother, my aunt Leonora, passed away, and I took my mother to Kansas City for the funeral. During the after-the-funeral thing where you have a bite to eat and everybody just visits, I had a chance to catch up with Cousin Clay. When he asked me about "that real estate stuff" I was doing, I just shrugged it off. Then he said, "You know, I wish you'd tell me more about what you're doing." In true secret-identity fashion I said, "This probably isn't the time or place to talk about all that." He said, "All right. I get it."

Clay had a gig that night, so I went to help him set up. We loaded the instruments and stuff into a beat-up minivan and drove to the diviest hole-in-the-wall bar in Kansas City. I know diviest isn't a word, but it ought to be; you should have seen this place! We were unloading all that stuff and my flip-flops were sticking to the floor because of all the spilled beer, and I was thinking, "This is really gross."

When we finished unloading, Clay asked me, "Are you ever going to share with me what you are doing with this real estate stuff?"

I felt cornered, so I just said, "I can... but how are you going to get involved?" Then Clay said, "Well, the house is completely paid off, and we don't have any debt at all. The girls are through college, two of them are married, and Shelly's living and working in Washington D.C. and has her own thing going on. I can't contribute any more of my money to my 401k because it's maxed out. Jeannie's IRA is maxed out, and honestly, Susan, you'd be helping me out because we're running out of places to put our money." OMG!! I felt like a real "Lassiter ass" for two reasons: One was because I'd judged him, and I still feel bad about that. The other was that I'd gone all that time without ever giving him the opportunity to partner with me, make money, and have some fun. It's a blast to invest with people you are related to!

That's Cousin Clay's story, and I promise you, chances are you have a "Cousin Clay" in your family. There's somebody close to you whom you're prejudging; somebody you think doesn't have any money; somebody whose feelings you don't want to hurt if they don't have the money to invest with you. For me it was Clay, and that's all on me. Who is it in your life? You know somebody with money. Don't you think they would benefit from safe, consistent returns?

The mind shift you have to make is that you are not borrowing money. It feels gross when you have to borrow money from someone because you feel like you're in this subservient, powerless position. Ditch all that. You are not asking somebody to borrow money. You are inviting them to partner with you in a real estate opportunity. That's the opposite of asking someone to borrow money; it's asking someone if they want to make money. Do you get it? Once this thing flipped in my mind, I was off to the races and you couldn't shut me up. I was talking to everybody I knew about opportunities to make them money.

Lost for Words; So What Do I Say?

I know you're probably thinking, "Okay, that's great. But what do I say to them?" How about this: "I just came across a great real estate deal and I have a partnership opportunity open. Do you want to grab a coffee or a margarita or a pedicure Friday and check it out?" (Psst, Ladies… this is a tip. You have a captive audience when you take somebody for a pedicure. Make sure that it is a "deluxe" so you spend extra time. They can't go anywhere. They're going to be sitting next to you for at least forty minutes!)

If they start asking you a bunch of questions while you're setting up the meeting, all you have to say is, "Those are all great questions, and I promise I will answer them all on Friday. What time do you want to get together?" You always want to meet with those people in person. If not, you'll be tangled up in the weird phone conversation thing, trying to answer their questions out of context. I'll detail how to structure presentation of the deal a bit later.

Bucket Two: Real Estate Investors

Bucket Two is people who are already investing in real estate. Where are they? They're at the Real Estate Investors

Association (REIA); they're on LinkedIn and Facebook. They're at meetup.com, a site you should get to know. Meetup is all about meetings for everybody about everything – and I mean everything. If you go to meetup.com and search for redheaded people with fourteen freckles on their right thigh who live in Denver, you'll find a group of ten who meet every Wednesday and – woohoo! – party with freckles! It's anything and everything. There are tons of real estate Meetups, too.

The REIA

The REIA is where I met the majority of my real estate partners, real estate investment partners, and funders. Here's what you say: "Tell me a little bit more about the kinds of deals you'd like to do." It's always best to start off with a question and not just pepper people with "So I put together lucrative real estate investing opportunities so my partners make safe, consistent profits." You might just be told to "Back off, Dude." Remember, this is a relationship business. You are building relationships that are usually created because you have some kind of shared interest with the other people. Start with a question: "What kind of real estate deals do you like to do?" When they tell you, ask them, "Have you ever thought about using some of your profits to fund other people's deals?" If they say yes, then say, "From time to time I have deals like that, or I come across people looking for funds for their deals. Would it be okay if I occasionally shared some of those deals with you?... Sure? Great! Let's trade contact information and go have a giant margarita sometime."

That's how I met my very first private money partner, Rick. He sat next to me at the REIA, and we started talking. I asked him what kind of investing he did, and he said, "I don't really do much anymore because I'm retired and I don't want to deal with all the work. I like to ride my bike." He rides in races like the MS150. I asked him what his dream opportunity would be, and he said, "It would be great if I could just turn my money over to somebody and they would just turn a profit and pay me interest or return my money to me. I want them to do all the work and make the money for me, and I don't have to do anything for it." I asked him, "How much are we talking?" His answer was, "Probably about $150,000."

The Investor's Lie

When you ask your potential private money partners how much money they have to invest with you, they will always lie to you. They will lie 100 percent of the time. It's okay, though; it's not a mean lie. It's just a little white lie. In fact, Rick had over $300,000 to invest, but investors aren't going to tell you the real amount because nobody wants to have all their eggs in one basket. Rick was not going to take his entire retirement account and turn it over to some flip-flop-wearing chick he met at the REIA. He was going to test me first. When I was successful with the deal, he said, "Now I've liquidated everything and here it is all for you. It's $330,000. Please put it to work. I have to go ride my bike." That's how it works. So just keep that little nugget in your pocket. Even your dad might be fibbing to you.

Bucket Three: The Big Fish

Let's go to Bucket Three: people who are already making private loans for real estate investors. These are the easiest people to find because all of the stuff they're doing is public information. You can get it for free off the internet, or you can pay somebody ten cents to give you the investor's name and address and the property address. Companies like ListSource. com have private lender records from all across the country that you can purchase. If you want to do it the free way, you can go to brbpub.com or publicrecordsources.com. Search by the county where your property is located or in an area where you want to invest. You can search by the document (mortgage or deed, for example) and input a date range. If your county only allows you to search by name, just input the first few letters of a common last name and search that way. Either way is going to return a whole bunch of data.

Granted, this is not the most efficient use of your time because it's point-click, point-click. As well, many of the documents refer to the usual suspects like Bank of America, Wells Fargo, and other assorted financial institutions. Occasionally you will get lucky and see an individual's name listed instead of a bank. When you find one of these – a deed of trust, for example – it will list the grantor (the borrower) and the grantee (the lender). It gives you the legal description of the property and, over on the left side, a blue clickable link where it says "Deed of Trust." Click on that, and boom! You are looking at a copy of the deed of trust and all the details of the loan.

You should not only be looking at individuals, but also at banks, entities, and trusts. Get the lender name or grantee; they're the private lender. Get the address, the loan amount, the date, and the property address. Focus on large, long-term, low-interest loans. You are not interested in the guy who's loaning $50,000 in second position at 18 percent; that's too expensive.

Portfolio Lenders; Search outside the Box

Here's a ninja tip: Because you are capturing entities and banks, you can also find the portfolio lenders we talked about in the previous chapter that are active in your area. They don't have to follow the conventions of Fannie Mae and Freddie Mac. With them you can have more than ten financed properties, you can do unseasoned cash-out refinances, construction loans, and even high loan-to-value (LTV) financing. One of my students found a portfolio lender close to the apartment building he was buying, so he got on a plane and flew there. He met with the banker and the loan committee (a grandpa, dad, and son) and was approved for 100 percent financing on the property. Portfolio lenders are valuable lenders.

Search your competitor's names in the public records in the counties in which they are located. Voila – an active lenders list. If you can get the members roster from your local REIA, start plugging in all those names. You just got a list of the active private lenders and the portfolio lenders in that area. Sweet!

ListSource; Mining the Mother Lode

Let's look at ListSource a little closer. It's free to get an account. Just go to ListSource.com and register. When you log in, you'll see a welcome page with a menu across the top with links for "Create Your Own," "Consumer Marketing," "Homeowner Services," etc. On the right-hand side there's a link called "Investor and Foreclosure Services." Click on it. In the attached drop-down box is a link called "Private Party Lender Prospects" that gives you a list of people in your target area who are actively making private loans on real estate. I would push that button a hundred times to Tuesday. Give me that list! You can get very specific in your search criteria, sorting by city, state, and county, and you can even drill down to certain neighborhoods. You can specify the property type or the amount of the loan. I did this recently to see how many prospects were listed.

Imagine my surprise when I found that in the U.S.A. in the last six months there were 180,265 private party loans recorded! That's a lot of potential candidates for Bucket Three, isn't it?

I've marketed to the lists in ListSource a lot, and these are the specific search criteria that worked best for me: Select your target county and state and then look for first mortgages. You want the leads with the lender names and addresses, but exclude seller carry-backs. Someone who is just carrying back didn't really loan money. You only want to find the loans from the last twelve months. Choose residential or commercial properties, depending on your interest. Sometimes I search on both so I can see who is loaning on what. Make the owner occupant status "absentee" to capture the records for loans made on investment properties. "Occupied" status often means a one-time deal. If Mom and Dad bought the newlyweds a house, chances are they're not going to invest with you. As far as "corporate owned" is concerned, choose "no preference" because you want to get hits showing the entities and trusts. A lot of prospects have self-directed IRAs that invest in an entity or trust. I like to see those because I can get the name of their trust or their LLC and then go to the local secretary of state website and search that name to see who's in that company and how to contact them.

That's my specific search criteria, and I encourage you to use it. What you'll get back is a table of data with a column listing the county and state you are searching. The next column is "Property Type," where it could list single family, duplex, triplex, apartments, and rural home sites. The "First Mortgage Lender Name" column lists the lenders; the next column their address; and their city. Now you have their contact information and you can market to them with a postcard. (I will be going through a specific strategy on exactly how to do that shortly.)

You Only Do This Once

Start to identify your private money prospects from all three buckets and create at least ten prospects you will speak to from each bucket. Bucket One is going to be as simple as making a list of people you know. Bucket Two could be as simple as going to your local REIA or starting up a meeting on Meetup. Filling Bucket Three is as simple as searching at ListSource. You now know how to find a ginormous list of them.

You need just thirty prospects to make this happen. You might need fewer. The good news is you don't need to go through this process every time you want to fund a deal. Once you get a private money partner, they're yours for life. As long as you treat them right, you get to continue to use that money over and over. I raised $26.2 million in private money, and I had twelve people on my list. That's all it took. To this day I have never had to search for another private money partner. That should make you feel a bit better about this process. If you do it right, you should only have to do it once. You can accomplish 95 percent of what you want to accomplish in your real estate investing business with just a handful of private money partners. I think that's good news.

Chapter Seven

STRANGER MARKETING

"Life begins at the end of your comfort zone."

–Neale Donald Walsch

We have gone over how to get those lists of Bucket Three private lenders, but what do you do once you get the list? You now know you can go to ListSource.com and look over a pool of 180,000 active private lenders across the United States. But how do you effectively contact them, communicate the details of your program, and start to build relationships with these people?

This is the stranger marketing element of finding money. The goal is to get these folks on your list. You have their names, you have their contact information, but you need them to join your list. To get them to join your wholesale buyer list, the conversation might go something like this: "I'm a real estate investor, and these are the types of deals that I do. You're investing in real estate and lending on real estate, and I often come across deals that I turn down. Would you like to be added to my wholesale buyers list to be notified of deals that I get?" Or you could just say, "From time to time I use private money like yours to fund my deals. Would it be okay if we got together so I could learn more about you and the types of deals that you like to fund?"

Are You on My List?

There is a core message here I want you to understand. The way you start to build and nurture these relationships and the way you finally get someone to decide to invest with you is with a simple conversation. That should be comforting to you. It's a big "aha!" moment for a lot of people when they realize it's not about a giant pile of paperwork or a formal presentation, it's just about asking. When you're asking these simple questions, be sure to encourage these people to "like" your Facebook page and check out your LinkedIn page, and by all means do everything you can to get their permission to add them to your email list.

You Sales Funnel; Down the Rabbit Hole

Your online lead generation starts with your website, then goes to your opt-in form, to your lead magnets, to your email list, to your phone call list, and then into your text messaging if you want to incorporate that platform. That's your six-step sales plan – your sales funnel. I want to make it very clear that the goal of the sales funnel and all the activities that make up this marketing plan is not to make a sale. The goal is simply to get the meeting. The concept is the same for the direct mail campaign that you're going to be using to reach out to people who are actively loaning private money. You have their names and their addresses, and you know the properties on which they've loaned. Spark their interest, get a call from them, and set the meeting to get to know them.

The Postcard; a Tap on the Shoulder

The postcard I send out says, "Your private money loan on [insert property address] made me realize we should talk."

Hmm, if I'm a private lender and I were to get this postcard in the mail, it would get my attention. Statistics tell us that of all the people who get direct mail pieces like postcards and letters, only 1 to 3 percent will physically pick up the phone and call you. This one is different. When I send out this postcard, the worst response has been about 12 percent while the best has been about 23 percent. This postcard gets results. Swipe it word for word or test your own, but this one works:

Your Private Money Loan on [Insert Property Address] Made Me Realize We Should Talk

My name is Susan, and I actively buy and rehab properties in Denver. Since you are already an active private lender, I thought we should talk for a few important reasons.

FIRST, I have more than 700 units across the country. Here's a little bit about my properties and partners:

www.YourDomain.com

SECOND, I have a large list of **experienced investors who pay people like you up to 10 percent for secured real estate loans** to buy, renovate, and sell distressed properties. I am not a mortgage or real estate broker, so I'm not trying to get fees by getting in the middle.

THIRD, I'd like to close more deals and know a conversation between us could be good. And, I would like to connect you, at no cost or obligation, to my list of investors so you can check out and maybe loan on more deals.

> *Send a direct e-mail to susan@yourdomain.com. Or, for more information, you can call my cell at 720 XXX-XXXX. If I don't pick up, please leave a brief message and I'll call you back soon.*

I'm not sending a postcard that makes me seem needy. I'm sending one that says, "I know who you are, and I have a couple of different ways that I might be able to help you." I'm leading with the value – the "what's in it for them?" It's not all me, me, me and "Let me tell you a little bit more about me" and "By the way, did you know this about me?" It's a super-important distinction.

Once you have created your postcards, automate the process of sending them out. When you have your ListSource contacts in an Excel™ spreadsheet, you can upload them to an online service like sendoutcards.com or click2mail.com. You upload the postcard template, push a button, and it will automatically do the sending for you. The cost is anywhere from fifty-eight cents to eighty-five cents, including postage, for each postcard you send.

The Forty-Five-Day Rule; Pleasure before Business

Let's talk about my "forty-five-day rule." The (SEC) wants us to have a pre-existing relationship with someone before we make an offer, solicit, or advertise to them about investing in our deals. Unfortunately the SEC has never specified what that pre-existing relationship should look like. I worked with an SEC attorney to come up with a good answer for this. Securities attorneys have job security forever because they're the ones who interpret these laws, guidelines, and rules for people like us. I needed assurance that I was doing everything I could to be in compliance with the SEC, so we came up with the forty-five-day rule.

From the first day I make contact with a potential private money partner, the clock is ticking. Over the course of forty-five days, I need to contact them a minimum of three times, and one of those times has to be a personal contact like a phone call or live meeting. Forty-five days; three touches. It can be an email, text message, voice broadcast, phone call, or in-person meeting, as long as one of those is personal. That is the best way to be able to demonstrate and document a substantive pre-existing relationship with your potential partner. The postcard you send out to investors is fine with the SEC as long as you are not inviting them to invest in a specific deal laid out in the mailing.

Digging for Common Ground

When these people call you (and they will), you might say to them, "Tell me a little bit more about the kinds of deals you like to do." Again, don't lead with your deal. You want to find out more about them because you're building a relationship. You can say, "From time to time I have investors looking for funding for their deals" or "I come across deals like you just mentioned. Would it be okay if on occasion I shared some of those deals with you?"

"Sure, that would be fine."

"Cool. What are you doing in your spare time?" "Well, I like to go fishing."

"Really? I like fishing, too." I don't, but this might be an example of something you could say to find that common ground.

Intelligence Gathering

Before you call, plug the name into Facebook and LinkedIn and Google to find out as much as you can about that person. Sometimes you can uncover some great information. I Googled one guy on my list and came across his family website. His family had a blog, so I read things like, "Here are the pictures from our last family reunion. Look at Cousin Bobby and how drunk he is. LOL" and "Our poor beloved German shepherd, Max, just died, and we're so sad."

I read an entire diary of this guy's life in chronological order for the last five years. I knew everything about him including his phone number because it was there, too. A lot of times you can get contact information from a Facebook business page or a LinkedIn page.

Get the Meeting!

Here is a sample of a phone script: "From time to time I use private money to fund my deals. Would you mind if I contact you occasionally with a few of the deals to take a look at?" Or even better: "Let's get together so you can tell me more about the types of deals you like to fund. By the way, I'm sorry about your German shepherd, Max. He looked awesome." That's the beginning of a relationship.

After you've met or had a conversation with them, and you have a deal you want to show them, you can say, "I just wanted to follow up with you. We chatted briefly about the investment opportunities our company provides. I wanted to see if you're interested in getting together to learn more about the types of deals we do." They're going to try to ask you a bunch of questions on the phone, but the goal of this phone call is not to sell the deal. The goal is to get the meeting.

You can deflect all the questions with, "Great questions; you're a little ahead of me, though. I have a short presentation I'd like to show you with some of the details about my company, the types of deals we do, and some of our successes. When would be a good time to get together?" You're not rude by not answering questions; you're just avoiding a situation in which you're not going to be able to explain it fully on the phone.

During the forty-five-day pre-existing relationship period, you can talk about generalities and the types of things you do and a little bit about your company, but you can't approach them with a specific deal or one on which you're currently working. The goal is to get them on your list. Again, going back to that credibility thing, you're credible because you're doing it. You're not going to meet or talk with them and have to worry about your credibility. First of all you just sent them a postcard saying, "I am a real estate investor. I'm doing it." That's instant credibility. And they called you. So there is no credibility issue. These people are making loans on deals. They're private lenders, and that's how they make money. They want more deals. But first they want to make sure you're a good fit for them before they jump on board. It's a two-way street.

Setting Up a Group

Remember meetup.com? If you go to meetup.com tonight and put in the search "private lenders, private lending, real estate lending, real estate loans" and search maybe twenty to fifty miles from your area, you might get lucky. You might find a group of people that meet on a regular basis to talk about things like that. You might get even luckier and there won't be a group! That means you get to start your own group. You can send a postcard to the people on your list and say, "My name is X. I noticed that you are actively lending on real estate in this area, and I'm putting together a Meetup group for private lenders so we can talk about deals and share information. Here's a link to my Meetup page where you can get information about where and when we're going to meet next." How cool would that be?

Here's an example: I set up a Meetup group that I called Profit Insights, Business & Automation. The name is weird and wordy, but I said, "I'm reaching out to other entrepreneurs who are doing business online in my area to say let's get together at this place near my house called the Punch Bowl." It costs you twelve dollars every month to have a Meetup organized at meetup.com. Can you afford to pay twelve bucks a month if you know that when you schedule events and invite private lenders to go have a cocktail or appetizers with you that maybe twenty of them would likely show up and you'd have a captive audience? Would that be worth twelve bucks?

Remember, you have credibility because you're doing this. They're not going to walk into the Meetup at the Punch Bowl, grab their beer, and come over and say, "So what's up with you? Have you even done any deals?" They're going to come over to you, shake your hand, and say, "I think it's so cool that somebody finally put this together. I'm excited to be here to get to know the other lenders in the area."

Everybody always assumes that if these guys are already making private loans on real estate, then they know the drill – that we can just give them a truncated version of what it is we're doing and that will be enough. It's not. Give them details on your program and the rates and the terms you can afford to pay. Share testimonials and information on previous deals and returns. Carrying a data card with a pic of a property and some telling data about one of your previous deals might come in handy. You can list the purchase price, the cash flow, the lender's investment, and their profit. That's all information that a potential investor would find very interesting. Show off your accomplishments!

Your Website: The Light at the End of Your Sales Funnel

A very important communication vehicle is your website. On the very first page people see, there should be a picture or video of you. People need to know you're real. Don't hide behind your website. Don't say "we" do this and "we" do that if it's just you. I know you want to say "we" because you want people to think you're a big company, but you are an "I." If you have a team, then it's "we," and you need to show a picture of the team. List your phone number and your email address and make it easy to contact you. Don't make it vague and make people wonder if there truly is somebody behind the hype. Be sure it's professional and clean and that you're updating the content often, especially if you have a blog. Have links to your Facebook business page and your LinkedIn profile. I could go on and on about your website and social media sites like LinkedIn and Facebook, and I probably should. They are the absolute best way to showcase your brand.

Chapter Eight

THE PRESENTATION

"Success is where preparation and opportunity meet."

−Bobby Unser

Let's talk about your private money presentation. You now know how to *identify* those private money partner prospects from the three buckets: the friends and family bucket, the people already investing in real estate bucket, and the people already making private loans on real state bucket. Now we are starting the *introduce* piece of the private money framework of *identify*, *introduce*, and invest.

Preparation; a Shot of Confidence

You've found a promising prospect and you've set up the meeting. How do you explain to them exactly what it is you're doing in such a way that it will get them interested in working with you? And how can you position yourself in such a way that your credibility will shine through?

First, never go into a meeting unprepared. Let's review what you have so far: You created your value statement and have something like "I put together lucrative real estate investments so my investors make safe, consistent returns." This particular value statement is a good one, and I see it everywhere now. That's okay. It wouldn't be out there if it didn't work.

You created your business plan. You figured out the mission statement of your company, your objectives, your strategies, and the tasks you need to do in order to accomplish those objectives and achieve that mission.

You created your private money program to determine the specific deals you are going to make based on your investment criteria and your analysis of the deal from both your perspective and your private money partner's perspective. What are your investment criteria? Do you want debt or equity partners? What is your rate of return? Do you need individual partners or a group of investors? What is your exit strategy? Extrapolate those answers, plug them into your private money presentation, and share them with your potential partners.

The Venue; Margaritas Are Better

I'm a huge fan of meeting with people personally, as you know, because I like La Loma and margaritas. If your investors are out of state and you can't just get on a plane and go meet with them, you can use a forum like Skype, Google Hangouts, or video chat. We have amazing technology available to us now so we can look somebody right in the eyeballs and talk to them in real time even though they might be in the Czech Republic or Ecuador. It's pretty amazing technology, but it's still Plan B. When you're communicating this information and determining whether or not you want to work with a private money partner, it's best to be sitting down right across from them. If you try to do this over email, you give the impression that you're scared and you're a wimp, and your business will never get off the ground. This is relationship financing. You're building a relationship so you can have these partners serve your business and make you money for years to come.

What I typically do is put together a brief PowerPoint presentation that goes over the big picture to get the initial buy-in. Then if the lender is interested, I share specific property details. I put all the numbers into ianalyzerei.com, and it spits out a fantastic, twenty- six-page professional presentation.

Customizing; Everyone Gets a Spin

I never give the same presentation to everybody. I like to demonstrate some alignment with my potential partner, so I customize each presentation to suit the potential partner. Over the course of the forty-five-day waiting period, I've taken the time to chat about what's important to them because I want to get to know them and find an alignment between us. If I know they are particularly concerned about neighborhood market values and they're into community and neighborhood revitalization, I lead with something like "What's important to you is important to me. I know that maintaining and even elevating market values in this area is important to you, and it's important to me, too. My company adds value to properties, to neighborhoods, and to people's lives. As an investor here, you'll benefit from the value we add and have a hand in changing your community for the better for everyone."

Solving Their Problem

Then I talk about the problem. I try to figure out some sort of issue that they have and let them know how I can solve it. For example: "The mortgage and foreclosure crisis has created a surge of discounted real estate opportunities here in Denver. Unfortunately it's also created volatility in traditional investments such as mutual funds, CDs, and stocks. Lots of people like you are really frustrated with the lower terms lately, right?" (That's a problem that they're having.) "Here's my solution. Our unique investment program offers quality investment opportunities backed by real estate to private investment partners just like you. Our partners rely on safe, consistent monthly cash flow or equity returns between X and X." I don't usually come out and say specifically what the term is, but give a range. I'll say, "They're anywhere from four to ten percent depending on the type of deal we're doing, and we pay monthly or quarterly."

The Coolness Factor

If there is a "secret sauce" to my presentations, I would say it's the coolness factor. It just means that I'm trying to find and share and get them excited about something cool in my investment. This stuff is pretty boring, right? We think it's cool, but when we share it with someone, it's like, "This is kind of boring. Can't we just have another margarita and watch the basketball game?" So what I try to do is figure out something cool about my investment and lead with that. There's a multi-family developer here in Denver called Boutique Apartments. Their buildings are the coolest multi- family properties in town. Each apartment building they develop has a theme. One of them has a movie theme and in the lobby there's a giant movie projector as a piece of art. I think they have a picture of Charlie Chaplain and some vintage actors on the outside. One of their apartment themes is outer space, and they have a rocket ship as a piece of art in the lobby. That's cool, right? I remember living in apartments when I was younger, and not one of my apartments was that cool. If given the choice, people would rather invest in a company that's cool than a company that's boring. All things being equal, would you prefer to invest in Apple or Campbell Soup Company? Soup's not that cool, right?

Executive Summary; A Chunk of the Plan

Next you're going to lead into an executive summary. You can extrapolate it right from your business plan. It can be something like, "We have an opportunity to acquire a one-hundred-and-fifty-six-unit, Class B apartment building in [whatever area] to hold for a minimum of five years, at thirty-five percent of the value, to rehabilitate and sell within one year." I want to give you a quick word of caution here. Unless you are presenting to someone from Bucket Three – people who are currently investing in real estate – you can lose your prospect by using real estate jargon. Be aware of who you're speaking with and adjust the complexity of the presentation to suit. Speak in plain terms when called for.

Project Overview; Brass Tacks

The project overview is a picture of the property, the cost, and the investment criteria. Tell them the total amount you need, the minimum amount you're accepting, and the term of their investment. Describe the exit strategy and the profit potential or estimated return on their investment.

You and Your Company

The next step is sharing a little bit about you and your company, and this is a great point at which to display your testimonials. You might be thinking, "But I haven't done a deal yet." The information you're going to share about your company is either your past accomplishments if you have them, or what you are planning to accomplish – your goals. That will be in the mission statement for your business and the objectives you've outlined in your business plan. Once you have done a few deals, then you get to tweak your presentation with testimonials.

Getting the Money

Chris, one of my coaching students, was a rehabber in Baltimore and a part-time DJ. Before he met me, he just decided one day to be a bar owner and DJ in his own club. By the time we met he was in a world of hurt. He had driven the bar into the ground and gone bankrupt. He's a great real estate investor, but he sucked at being a bar owner. I helped him get back into the game, but the bankruptcy scared him. People are afraid that because they've never done a deal before, or have been bankrupt, or have been invited for "a chat" as the target of an SEC investigation, nobody will deal with them. I convinced Chris to pursue his plan, and the people he presented to didn't say, "I'm not going to invest with you because you ran that bar into the ground and you had to file for bankruptcy." They invested with him because they could see what he had accomplished with real estate. Even though he disclosed his bankruptcy to every single person he worked with, nobody cared.

Partner Benefits; What in It for Them?

The next part of your presentation is *partner benefits*. The biggest mistake you can make here is to make it all about you: "I did this; I did that; and I'm so very great. Here are pictures of me, here's my dog and my house, and here's my car. Here's me drinking a margarita. Here's me, me, me, and here's a little bit more about me." Nobody wants that. They like you and they're happy to be in this relationship with you, but now they want to know what's in it for them in terms of this investment. Talk about proven performance if you have a documented record of success. Talk about how your plan is an effective approach to wealth-building. Put a slide up that shows some stats: "Real estate is the #3 billionaire-maker globally." When people want to diversify, real estate is one of the things they look at, but they often don't know how to do it. Your friends and family especially don't know how to do it, though they know it's a good wealth diversification and accumulation strategy; they know real estate is a tangible asset.

Outline how your investors benefit from real estate tax advantages. You get cash-flow, appreciation, depreciation, and equity. That was the whole reason I got involved in real estate in the first place. I invested and did pretty well in stock-options trading, and then I pretty much lost every penny when I had to pay the tax bill at the end of the year because of all the short-term capital gains. I needed a tax shelter, so I started looking at real estate. People understand these types of concepts, especially high-net- worth individuals.

The Call to Action; Their Next Step

The final part of your presentation is a call to action. I look over lots of presentations, and the call to action is often missing – and it's so important. Tell them what you want them to do! People have pitched me before using this very template. When they get to this point they just look at me and say, "So what do you think?" That's the kiss of death. I don't care what my potential investors think because it's my job to tell them what to think. This deal is mine and I'm not going to ask them for their thoughts. I'm going to say, "If you want to partner with me, this is exactly how you do it and what you must do right now to make that happen." Then define the investment details. Talk about the amount they need, the timeframe during which you will be using the money, and the payment terms. Prepare a simple loan offering, position the funds for availability, prepare the investor paperwork, and deliver funds to closing. (I'll show you this process later in the book.)

The Five "Must Answer" Questions

There are five questions your potential partners will have even if they don't ask them. Be sure to answer all five of these questions during the course of your presentation. The first is "What is it?" Explain the deal in common terms that they can understand. Instead of a "multi-family acquisition," just say, "We're going to buy an apartment building." That's what it is.

The second question is "How much do you need?" "We're raising two million, but you can get in for as little as fifty thousand."

The third question is "How much can I make?" Show them the range of returns they can make or the profitability of previous projects similar to this one. They're going want to know when they get their money back, so address that in the terms.

The fourth question is "What if I need to get my money back before then?" I usually write the answer into my offering and explain, "This is a five-year deal, and I hope that you're going to be in with us for the whole five years to make the biggest return, but I know things happen. So you're going to commit your money to us for at least a year. If after that year something happens and you need to cash out your shares and get your money, here's what happens: The other members of this investment have first right of refusal, meaning we have the first option to buy your shares. I will ask the other members if they want to buy your shares. I've only had this happen once, and the other investors said, 'Hell yes, we want the shares.' If the other members of the investment don't want them, they have approval over whom you sell your shares to." The group would want to make sure that the new investor is a suitable fit for the group. As the manager, if you have enough cash on hand you can buy the shares yourself. There are lots of different ways to do that.

The fifth question might seem a little morbid, but I learned the hard way that I need to provide the answer whether they ask or not. When I first started out and kept getting no for an answer, I sought out feedback to find out what I was doing wrong. One of the biggest things I heard was, "You never told me what would happen if something happened to you. I like you and trust you, but you could get hit but a bus tomorrow, and then what happens?" Be sure you have a plan and answer this question in advance. Write it into the offer. You can appoint someone to wind up operations if something happens to you, or you can buy a life insurance policy and direct the proceeds to go to an attorney who will take over operations and wind down the asset or investment. There are lots of different ways to structure it, but let your prospects know how they will get their money back.

Those are the mechanics of the presentation. Now it's time to draft your presentation. If you're raising money for a specific deal, craft your presentation around that deal. If you've identified your specific investment criteria, craft it around those criteria. Practice your presentation on three people. It doesn't have to be three prospects from your buckets; it can be your spouse, your partner, or your neighbor. Ask for feedback. The only way to get comfortable with it is to practice.

Chapter Nine

THE PSYCHOLOGY OF THE PRESENTATION

"The person who owns the frame owns the conversation."

–Oren Klaff

You've put together a PowerPoint outline of your deal and included all the elements we talked about in the previous chapter. But there's another element at play when you present your offer. Your presentation is essentially a negotiation, and there is always a psychological component in negotiating with someone. Here are some things to consider when you are presenting your deal:

Rapport; There's Nothing like a Good Connection

Rapport is the harmonious connection that exists when two or more people are on the same wavelength or relate well to each other. People who want to be in business with you want to be able to relate to you and feel some rapport with you. You might think you can keep your presentation at the cold, hard, math level, but people don't like being treated that way.

The Good Spy

Know your prospect. That's why I said to never make the same presentation twice. Spy on people; not in a weird NSA way, recording their phone calls or something – but just check them out. Google or Facebook them to learn about their interests or hot-button issues. On my Facebook profile I'm kissing a dolphin. That says something about me. Hopefully it says something good and not something bizarre. Start with a compliment: "That is such a cool picture of you kissing the dolphin on your Facebook page." People say that to me all the time and I love it. I say, "That was in Mexico, and her name was Olean and she weighed five hundred pounds and she was a great dancer." "Ha-ha-ha." Start off with something funny that breaks the ice.

Active Listening

Practice active listening. Listen carefully to what your prospects say and take exact notes. They will bring up objections and concerns, and you can overcome those by restating. Restate their concerns, objections, and questions in words that get them to look at the other side of the equation. It's a powerful technique. When I worked as a national sales trainer at Hertz's corporate headquarters, I traveled around the country and taught the counter representatives how to sell the insurance and all that extra stuff that nobody wants to buy. When a customer said, "No, I don't need that," I would restate, "So what you're saying is that your insurance will cover it? No? Well just to be sure, you should probably sign up." The same thing works in your presentation. When your prospect says, "I think I like my money better in the stock market," you say, "So what you're saying is that because you're investing in preferred stocks, you believe that the value will never go to zero." Once you get agreement you can move forward and address the objection.

The No-Cash Objection; Empty Pockets

You will come up against two basic objections. They can phrase them a thousand different ways, but every single objection comes down to either they have no cash or they have no faith. The no- cash objection is fixable, and the no-faith one is all on you. It's your job to figure out which issue is the problem.

If they say to you, "I'd love to invest with you, but you said the minimum investment is $100,000, and I'm just not that liquid right now," you say, "What you're saying is if you had $100,000 liquid that you'd be in?"

"Well, sure."

"All right, cool. Let's figure out how we can get you that cash."

"Cool."

"There's this really cool thing that you can do which is roll over your IRA or your 401k into a self-directed IRA, so you get to invest in things other than the mutual funds in which they say you have to invest. You'd be able to invest in my deal and grow that money tax free. How's that sound?"

"I've never even heard of that before."

"It's awesome, right? Let me hook you up with my rep at iDirect Law, and he'll walk you through the process and we'll see if that's something you're interested in."

Here are four more ideas to liquidate assets: certificates of deposit, stocks or bonds, home equity lines of credit, and stock loans. I have detailed information about stock loans in the Getting the Money home study program that you should take a look at. There are companies out there that will make loans against someone's existing stock portfolio that are non-recourse, and they don't even have to liquidate the stocks. And there is always cash.

The No-Faith Objection; Empty Heart

What if your prospect's faith in the deal is not solid enough to sign with you? Here's one solution you can offer: When I was brokering private money I might say, "This deal's great. I've underwritten it, and it's a $180,000 investment. The borrower's solid and I want you to put your money in it."

Then I might hear, "It looks to me like the guy is already doing two other deals simultaneously, and I'm just not feeling that great about it."

I would say. "What you're telling me is if the deal were a little bit more secure, you'd be in?"

"Yes."

"I got you. Let's do a Collateral Repurchase Agreement that says if this deal starts not performing the way it's supposed to, I will buy it back from you." How could I do that? Just get another private money partner and swap them for the waffler. I've done a Collateral Repurchase Agreement three times in all these years, and have never had to repurchase the collateral because the deals never went south.

Partner with experience. Remember I said it's always best to find a partner who's strong where you're weak. What can you do when they call your lack of experience into question? What if they say, "I think it's great that you're doing this real estate thing, and I want to support you, but I don't want to be the first guy at the party. You should cut your teeth and get some experience under your belt, and then let's talk."

Your response: "So what you're saying is that if I had more experience and had a couple of deals under my belt, you'd be in?"

"Absolutely."

"Let me tell you about my partner in this venture, Jim. I'm raising the money and managing the project, but I'm also learning from him because he has been a rehabber in this market in these exact types of properties for the last twelve years. Here are some pictures of the properties he has remodeled. He's also a general contractor, and he has his own crew. He's going to be the one making this happen. Want to meet him?"

That's called *partnering* with your *credibility*. If you think you have a credibility problem, find somebody who has that credibility and partner with them. Do you see how that changes the conversation?

Another option is to have a paid advisory board. If credibility is an issue, say, "Though this deal is my first right out of the gate, I've put together an advisory board. I have a general contractor, a syndicator who has years of experience in this asset class, a securities attorney who's guiding me in preparing the documents, and a real estate coach who's been doing this for the last nineteen years. Here is some information about them." I think that makes your package a heck of a lot stronger from a credibility perspective.

If you feel like you have a credibility issue, or maybe you're still stuck in your secret identity, find somebody who is strong where you're weak to partner with you so you can get your feet wet.

Get a couple of deals under your belt, and then instead of saying, "This is what I'm going to do," you can say, "This is what I have done." You might have to give up a significant amount of the profits right out of the gate to bring a partner on board, but it's worth it.

Scarcity; Last Chance!

Scarcity is when people want more of something than is available – the demand is greater than the supply. When something is scarce, it has more value. That's how scalpers make a living; when a game is sold out, ticket prices go up and good seats become a treasure. We can inject scarcity into our presentations using deadlines, because deadlines close deals. The fear of losing something is powerful. You might say, "We're only accepting one new investment partner this month, so if you want to get in, you'll need to get on it," or "We'll have a partner lined up to fund this deal by Monday, so if you're interested, you'll need to act fast," or "I have two more meetings this week with investors, and only one deal available. I hate it, but if you don't commit today, you're going to lose this opportunity."

Five Presentation Flaws

Let's go over five presentation flaws. These come from what we've discussed above. The first is giving too much detail too soon. I used to try to front-load my presentations with graphs and charts and numbers and all sorts of this and that; I was teaching trigonometry that made their heads explode. If they don't understand it, their automatic reaction is always going to be no.

The second is a presentation that is too vague or convoluted. If you can't clearly articulate what it is you're investing in or what your company is doing, you're going to lose them. That's why I focus so much on getting as specific as you possibly can with your investment criteria.

The third presentation flaw is not having a strong call to action. Tell your prospect exactly what to do next. Don't assume they will act – facilitate their action! "If you want to get in on this deal, this is what you need to do."

The fourth presentation flaw is not having a coolness factor – no secret sauce. If you don't do your research and don't know how to structure your deal so it piques the interest of your prospect beyond the rate of return, you are setting yourself up for failure.

The last presentation flaw is neediness. Don't come across as needy. Neediness comes from inferiority. It's the feeling that you are a very small mouse stepping into a very large snake pit to borrow a few crumbs. You are relying on pity and the generosity of others to keep your business alive. Reframe your thinking to put yourself on even ground with whomever you are dealing with, even if they treat you like you are beneath them.

Busting Frames

Oren Klaff is a professional money-raiser who wrote a book called *Pitch Anything*. He has raised several billion dollars for all sorts of different companies and projects. He's a badass when it comes to making a presentation. In *Pitch Anything* he talks about the concept of frames – personality types. He says that the person with the strongest frame wins. There's the "power" frame and the "authority" frame, among others. He talks about ways you can bust those frames. If you've ever been in a situation in which you go into somebody's office and they wave you into the seat and barely look at you while they sit behind their giant desk, then you have an idea what a power frame looks like; they just continue talking all their important talk and ignore you, demean you, and treat you like you are inferior to them. It doesn't feel good, right? That's why I never go to someone else's office to share my opportunity with them. No way. La Loma or nothing. I want control over the environment.

To clarify this concept of frames, imagine you're driving down the road, minding your own business, and you look in your rear-view mirror and see lights flashing and hear the siren. The cop's coming up fast, and you're thinking, "Is he coming for me? What did I do? Was I speeding? What's happening? Am I going to get pulled over?" At first you're not sure it's you he wants, but then he comes right up to your back bumper and hangs there, offset so he fills up your rear-view and side mirrors. He's in your space – a noisy, flashing, government-issued space invader. There's no doubt he wants you, so you pull over. Does he get out of his car right away? No. He sits there and gives you time to feel the weight of the law. When he walks up to your car, his pace is slow and measured. His aviator sunglass frames match his shiny badge, and he's all about his power frame. You have to roll down your window, and he's got his gun, right? That's some power, and it's very intimidating.

Most of us faced with that situation can hear our hearts beating out of our chests. We're shaky as we scramble for our insurance card and our driver's license. And we're praying, "Please let me have my registration in here." We become a fumbling, nervous, sweaty mess when all those weird physiological reactions happen in our bodies.

This exact thing happened to me at the beginning of my recent Cape Cod trip. I had bought a brand new Audi Q5, and I think I only had 250 miles on it when I left. I was still in Colorado on a pretty desolate road, doing almost 100. I love my new car; it drives nice and smooth. All of a sudden this kid came up fast and blew by me. If I was going 100, I don't even want to know how fast that kid was going. Next thing I know, I see lights in my rear- view and a cop passes me and pulls the kid over. As I was about to pass them, the cop stepped out into the middle of the highway and pulled me over, too. "Oh crap." So I pulled over. I had never seen that before, and I thought it was kind of cool the way he got a twofer. I bet that made his day. I rolled down my window and got all my stuff, and the cop comes up to me in his power frame.

Then a funny thing happened. I started talking to him about the Audi and some of the bells and whistles it came with and that it's a wireless hotspot, and his whole power frame shattered. I cracked a couple of jokes and treated him like he was human, and he became human. He started telling me about another lady driving a Q5 he had pulled over, and asked me more about the car. I completely busted his power frame. He gave me a ticket, but reduced the violation. He was cool about it because I had busted his frame.

Take that control away from them. If you can't bust their frame with humor and the human touch, instead of just sitting there and waiting patiently and letting them treat you that way, shut your portfolio or whatever you have with you, pick up your stuff, say, "Thank you for your time," and leave. Nobody has time to be treated like that.

Prizing

Oren Klaff also talks about prizing extensively in his book. Here's the Cliff's Notes version: "Prizing is the act of shifting or reframing the selling environment so the buyer sees you as a prize that he must win." It involves three principles. The first is realizing that humans possess a hunter mentality. They desire things that are moving out of reach. Klaff says, "We want that which we cannot have and we only place value on things that are difficult to obtain." If you don't present yourself as the prize that everyone wants to get, you will appear to be soft and weak, hiding in the buyer's shadow; you will only get to do business when, out of pity, someone tosses a few crumbs.

The second prizing principle is to realize that money is a commodity. That's all it is. If you want more of it, spend less. Sell some of the crap you've accumulated over the years, and you will have more.

Klaff says, "It may be hard to get meetings where buyers give you their money, but ultimately, that's all they have, money … You should never compromise your price, your time, your values, and certainly not your fun to get this plentiful commodity … Once you believe that money is a commodity, the right words will tumble from your lips. 'I only work with good customers that are fun, and they let me profit. What kind of customer are you?' That's what you'll be saying."

The third principle is to eradicate your neediness. When you're speaking, you can tell when someone (or a group) starts to lose interest in what you're saying. They look at their watch, fidget in their chair, or get a glazed look in their eyes. Your natural reaction is to try harder, talk louder or faster – anything to get them back. Klaff says, "The more we want the buyer to validate us, the more neediness we broadcast, the less likely they are to give us what we want. There's a name for this. Engineers call this the negative feedback loop." A negative feedback loop can cripple a power grid and even destroy buildings. It's not hard to imagine how it could destroy your presentation and your deal. Don't be needy. You are not looking for money, you are seeking the right fit for your deal.

You Are the Prize

Do you recognize any themes? We talked about neediness being one of the big flaws in pitching. We only want to work with fun customers who are going to let us profit. You are the prize. Money is a commodity. I love his comment "Money is all they have." You have everything else, and money is a commodity. Once you start realizing that you are the prize, you are going to start presenting a little bit differently and thinking a little bit differently about you and your position in all of this.

You are looking for partners. You don't want bad partners. You don't want asshole partners. You don't want partners who are going to waste your time and make your life miserable. You want fun partners. Because at the end of the day, this is your business… don't you want to have some fun?

I'm friends with my investment partners. I've had these friends for a long time. We go to basketball games. We go to football games. We see each other at barbecues. We go to parties and Super Bowl parties together. We involve ourselves in each other's lives. If you're going to have these people involved in your deal and involved in your life, recognize that you are the prize. The only thing they bring is money, and they better come with something else if they're going to get lucky enough to be your partner. You can do this. You have to believe in your deal. You have to believe in yourself. Because I'm going to say it again and keep saying it: you are the prize. Project your confidence and ditch the neediness. You're not begging for a loan; you're presenting someone with the opportunity to make money and get the prize. If they don't see the value in that, "Next!" Don't beg.

Practice restating and overcoming common objections, and more important, all you really have to do is listen. Just listen to what the people are saying. Have great conversations with them. And if it seems like you could work together and there is some alignment there, then move forward. If you're getting that feeling in your gut that this just isn't going to work out for you, move on. There's always another investor right around the corner.

Practice frame-busting. The next time you get pulled over, bust that power frame and see how good it feels. Start taking charge of situations in which you ordinarily wouldn't. You can do this!

Chapter Ten

CLOSING THE DEAL

"If you start it, finish it. Don't leave loose ends and unfinished business. Be a woman or man of your word."

–Anonymous

You've found a money partner, you've made the presentation, and your partner has agreed to invest with you. How do you close the deal? The process itself is pretty much the same every time: Prepare the loan package and schedule the closing. Then prepare the closing instructions for the title company or the closing attorney, and arrange for the funds to be wired. File whatever state forms you need to file. If you are a member of the Getting the Money online program, you can download all the documents you need from the site. The site also has a link to every state's requirements for closing. Typically you will need a Form D, which is a simple form to fill out, or a Form U2 which in effect says, "Here's my address in case somebody wants to sue me." Then set up the investment partner and property files.

The Loan Package

First up is the loan package. It consists of a promissory note and a mortgage or deed of trust, depending on whether yours is a mortgage state or a deed of trust state. As the borrower working with a debt partner, you have to take control of this process, especially when you're dealing with someone from Bucket One or Bucket Two who has never made a private loan before. I couldn't have said to Rick after he gave me the first $150,000, "Cool. Prepare the docs, and I'll see you at closing." He would have said, "What the heck does that mean? What do I have to do? What do I prepare?" With one-to-one transactions I typically take responsibility for this. If you're working at a super-high level with millions of dollars and multiple investors, you might have your attorney prepare these documents.

A promissory note is one party's written promise to pay another party a particular sum of money either on demand or at a specified time in the future. You can download promissory notes from your realtor commission website, or we have sample promissory notes you can download from the members' area at Getting the Money. You can also get them from FannieMae.com online.

The mortgage or deed of trust is the debt instrument. It's secured by the property, and you're obliged to pay it back according to the terms that you specify and agree upon with your private money partner in the promissory note. Mortgages and deeds of trust can be downloaded from the same sites, including our members' area. They're very easy to complete; just fill in the blanks.

You might need an LLC resolution. You should be borrowing in the name of your entity, so you should already be in an LLC. If you haven't written into your operating agreement that you have the authority to borrow money on behalf of your LLC, you will have to fill out this little form. It says, "I can sign for a loan and take on financing on behalf of the LLC." Again, samples can be found on the website. We've got everything there for you.

Insurance; Your Added Security

I recommend having a title insurance policy and a hazard policy. You should have an owner's policy in the amount of the purchase price to protect you against title defects. It will last as long as you own the property. You should also have a lender's policy to protect your private money partners. It's for the loan amount only, and it protects the lender for as long as the loan is in place. This stuff is super-expensive, but is extra security that you can offer your private money partner.

Hazard insurance is like a homeowner's policy, but it's on your investment property. Your hazard insurance policy names your lender as the loss payee. The piece of paper that says, "Yes, we agree to insure you," is called a binder, and you get that at closing. Let your hazard insurance agent know that the loss payee or the mortgagee (those two terms are used interchangeably) for the policy is your private money partner or your lender. If the property burns down, a tornado knocks it down, or flood waters carry it off into the ocean, the check doesn't come to you; it goes directly to your private money partner.

The Disclosure Document; What You Say Is What You Do

You can write a disclosure into your promissory note, in a separate addendum, or in your private placement memorandum. Whichever way you structure it, the disclosure document should include a few key points. First, the business of the company from your business plan – something as simple as "We are in business to do X." Second, risk factors. Real estate is a risky business that can be affected by market downturns, a new competitor, etc. Third, how you will use the proceeds. Fourth, key personnel involved in the deal. And fifth, any exemptions used. Each state has particular exemptions such as you're exempt from registering your security or your offering with the SEC. A list of state exemptions can be found at the members' area of Getting the Money.

An example of an exemption is the one for Colorado. It's in the Colorado Statutes S.11-51-308 1i, and sounds very official. All it says is that you can offer this deal to no more than twenty people, and you can sell it to no more than ten. There's no filing requirement. I don't have to file anything with the State of Colorado as long as I'm under these limits. It goes on to say that there is no legend requirement. Legends are special wording that say something like "This is a security" or "This is not a security and there are no rights or guarantee of ..." If your state requires a legend, our Getting the Money list will tell you exactly what you have to write. Compliance is as simple as copying the wording and pasting it into your disclosure document.

Record-Keeping and Your Master Inventory List

Record-keeping is important, and it's a requirement. You should keep a file for each of your investors and private money partners. Your records should include an executed (signed) *investor questionnaire*. You can find a sample at our website. Your records should also include an executed *subscription agreement*. A subscription agreement is a commitment. It's a document that your investors sign saying, "I have $X and I'm committing that amount to your deal." Your records should also include a copy of the promissory note and a copy of the check or wire that your private lender sent to the title company or closing attorney. If you are required to file form D or U2, keep a copy in the file. Include a copy of the master investor list or spreadsheet.

You don't need an expensive software program to create a master investor list. All you need is a spreadsheet that lists their name, address, phone number, and email address. I list exactly how much they have available in private money, titled "Total Capacity." It's their total capacity for lending. I also list how much they have outstanding with me and how much they have left over or available for me, and any notes I want to include. I use this list to keep track of birthdays and anniversaries so I can send cards or commemorate anniversaries of deal closings. It's a celebration, and it's a nice touch.

Closing Instructions; Heads Up

You will need to send *closing instructions* to the title company to explain what's happening in the transaction. Tell them what checks to cut out of the closing proceeds including insurance, rehab cost, and appraisal fees. Let them know you want to approve the HUD- 1 settlement statement (the debt instrument) before they fund the deal, which outlines how the money is going to flow and where all the money is going to go. Let the title company or closing attorney know if you'll be bringing the loan documents (the promissory note and the deed of trust or mortgage) or if you want them to prepare them. I personally prefer to prepare my own note and deed of trust and then have the title rep or the closing attorney look them over just to make sure I haven't missed anything. The title company files the deed of trust or mortgage. The original note doesn't have to be notarized; it usually stays with the lender until you pay it off.

Don't file the HUD-1 yourself. Let the title company or the closing attorney do that. I made the mistake of filing one in the wrong county. I was the private lender in a transaction in which I loaned $26,000 to a borrower (I'll call him Bob) in second position. I'd done four or five deals with him, and even though I don't normally lend in second position, I felt okay about it because of the relationship I had with him. Because I owned a mortgage company, I offered to handle the closing. But instead of filing the lien document in Denver County, I mistakenly filed it in Arapahoe County. When he sold the property, the title company missed my lien. When the deal closed, I didn't get paid off. Bob should have noticed when he looked at the HUD-1 that he was getting an extra $26,000, but he didn't. Unfortunately I had to get all Tony Soprano on him. I called him and said, "I need my $26,000." He said, "I'm sorry about that. I had to put it into another deal. So you can just transfer your lien to that property." I said, "I don't want to be in that deal, and I don't want to be in a deal with you anymore because you're a liar. Our relationship is over. You have until the end of the day to bring me my $26,000." He didn't show up.

The next week I was sitting in my office trying to figure out what to do, when I got an email from another guy announcing a new condo development in Crested Butte he was showcasing with his partner Bob. The email was an invitation to view the plans and pre-order a condo. They were going to serve champagne and strawberries and lobster. I read the email with one eyebrow raised. "Is that right?" It was a fancy-schmancy deal, so I called up the other guy and said, "So I see that you're having a big soiree down in Crested Butte next weekend. And I see that your partner is Bob." He said, "Yes." I said, "Bob owes me $26,000. So I'm going to come to your soiree and let everybody know precisely what he did in my transaction unless you pay me my $26,000." There was a pause on the other end. Then he said, "Let me call you back in ten minutes." Click.

He called me back and said, "I'm going to pay you the $26,000 because I don't want any bad blood around this new development. But I'm leaving town today and I have to be at the airport at one. I'll get you the money when I come back." I said, "Nope. Not good enough. I'll meet you there at the gas station on the corner of Pena Boulevard." I was there with my tire iron within reach. He brought me a cashier's check for $26,000 and the transaction went down in the parking lot of a gas station near the airport.

An interesting side-note and follow-up is that Bob, Fraudie McFraud, ended up filing bankruptcy. Because it was Bob's partner who paid me that $26,000, the bankruptcy trustee couldn't touch it. So this is a lesson about integrity and due diligence. More to the point, let the professionals do your filing, because sometimes even the smallest mistake can have huge ramifications.

The following is a sample of simple closing instructions:

MEMO

Date: April 12, 2005

To: Derek Sanner – Metro Denver Title (via email)

From: Susan Lassiter-Lyons

RE: Closing Instructions for Lassiter #1 – File No. 05-03-431

Hey Derek,

Here are the closing instructions for the above referenced transaction. A wire in the amount of $196,000 is scheduled to arrive prior to our scheduled closing at 1:00pm Thursday April 14th at your office. Please disburse the following:

Legal Fees	$350	Payable to: Carpenter & Klatskin, P.C.
Insurance	$839	Payable to: The Cambridge Group, Ltd.
Rehab Draw	$14,000	Payable to: Susan Lassiter-Lyons
Total	$15,189	

I will bring the loan documents. The deed of trust is 6 pages.

Please email a HUD-1 to me at susan@lassitermortgage.com for approval. Please let me know if you have any questions.

See you Thursday!

It's just a simple email, or you can write it up in a memo and attach it to an email. Send it to the closing attorney or the title rep. I had an attorney prepare some documents for me, and he charged me $350. Did I pay the amount out of my pocket? No, I paid it from the money that my private money partner was wiring and loaning me. It was part of the loan transaction.

I told Derek I would bring the loan documents, and because there is a fee for each page of the deed of trust I told him how many pages he needed to charge me for so it would be accurate on the HUD-1 settlement statement. The notice simply tells him that there is some money coming and where it needs to go.

Your Investor's Money Is Not for You

Now you're getting the money for real. It's time to have your private money partner fund the deal. You call them up and say, "Partner, it's time. Wire the money to the title company (or the closing attorney)." Provide the wiring instructions you get from the closer. *Wiring instructions* is just a fancy way to say "bank account information." If your money partner has checkbook control, they can just cut a check to the title company. Those funds go into escrow, which means the title company holds them until it actually makes those disbursements and the deal funds. Never have your private money partner cut the check directly to you. Never! You want the title company or closing attorney to record the disbursements so there is a formal money trail in case there are questions about it later from an investment partner, or worse, an SEC investigator.

People try to do all sorts of crazy things. I had a coaching student from Canada named Chris. He ended up getting a million dollars from his neighbor. The neighbor said, "I've got a million bucks. I have to liquidate some things but let me cut you a check for a hundred thousand right now." The neighbor cut him a check for a hundred grand and Chris put it in his bank, which meant that he had to start paying interest immediately on money that wasn't invested in a deal yet. I had to tell him to give it back immediately. When we find someone who is ready to pay us, our brains get flooded with hormones and we can forget the basic principles. Don't let your money partner pay you directly!

The Closing Letter

When you accomplish whatever it is you wanted to accomplish with your property, the title company or closing attorney will need a *payoff statement* to pay off your private money partner when you sell or refinance. It's a letter written on behalf of your investor that lets the title company or the closing attorney know exactly how much money your private money partner is entitled to. Provide the property address, the loan number, the lender's address, and the loan type (I always just put "conventional"). Say that this payoff is good through whatever date, and provide the principal balance, the accrued interest, and the total loan to be paid off. What you're saying is "Here's what we owe today, and if it closes in a week here's the amount of additional interest that's going to accrue that you'll need to tack on." I always provide a per diem interest rate. In the event of a delayed closing, they can use that rate to calculate the interest and add it to the payoff. Have your private money partner sign the letter, and fax it to the title company or the closing attorney. Your private money partner can go to the closing if they want to and get their cashier's check right there, or they can have it sent directly to them. That is the whole closing process.

Releasing the Lien

Once the loan pays off, don't forget to release it. That's another mistake I made once. I paid off a loan to Rick and then went on to my next deal. Everything went fine until the title company representative said, "We can't do this closing because we show that you still owe money on this other deal. No one has released the lien. You can't sell it unless you pay off this guy." I said, "I already paid him off." They said, "He hasn't released the lien, so we have to delay closing." Nobody had told me about that, so I'm telling you now to be sure you release the lien.

If you tell your private money partner that they need to file a *release of lien*, chances are they're going to scratch their head and say, "I don't know what that means." So have your servicing company prepare the release for them, or help them yourself. The county needs to be notified by the lender so it can release the lien. You can usually just download and prepare an e-file that can be sent to the county online. I have a sample lien release for you in the Getting the Money members' area. The title company will often handle the release, but if you are paying your partners without a title company you will need to take care of the release.

That's it. That's how you close your deal. Now you are ready for the next one!

Chapter Eleven

TENDING THE GARDEN; MANAGING YOUR PRIVATE MONEY PARTNERS

"The best time to make friends is before you need them."

—Ethel Barrymore

The Value of One Investor

It's time to talk about how to manage your beloved private money partners. I firmly believe that all lasting business is built on friendship. I prefer to do business with people who are my friends, who are in alignment with me, and who are fun to hang out with. Making friends is fun.

Let's talk about the lifetime value of just one of these private money partner relationships. We'll use Rick, a real-life example – my very first private money partner who had $300,000 available for me. When I met Rick, the reason I wanted to use his money was because I was tired of making tiny profits on tax-lien and lease-option deals and making peanuts on the spread. I wanted the financing so could I make big bucks on my deals. So I started rehabbing residential multi-family units using only Rick's money. My average price point on these deals was $150,000, and my profit after flipping them was around $25,000 for a six-month turnaround. Four deals a year netted me $100,000 annually without having to use a penny of my money or credit or doing anything but helping him with the logistics. How would you feel if you could make $100,000 in a year just doing four deals with somebody else's money? Would it feel good? Take it from me, it feels great. If I had decided to continue to do that for ten years, I would have made $1 million from one private money partner who had just $300,000. How would that feel?

The point is that you don't need a ton of investors to be successful in your investing business. You can do it with one partner; just one. For the $26.2 million in deals funded over the course of my ventures, I used twelve people. And those twelve are still with me today saying, "We're ready for the next deal whenever you want us." How does that feel? It feels awesome.

Who Are Your Profit Multipliers?

The key to success in this business is relationships. Your relationships are what I call your "profit multipliers" – from private money partners to appraisers, inspectors, realtors, insurance agents, attorneys, title company reps, contractors, buyers, coaches, and lenders. These are the people who support your business and allow you to make your profits. These are the people who warn you against bad deals and give you heads-ups about value issues. They let you know, "Hey, maybe you're overlooking this" and "Hey, don't forget about that." Every single one of these relationships can impact your bottom line. That's why you need to develop them, treat them well, and nurture them. You don't want to be a hit-and-run investor.

The Relationship Framework

I love frameworks. I'm a geek. I put together a relationship framework that I think is pretty accurate. Relationships start with a *formation phase* during which you identify your profit multipliers. Then there's the performance phase, and then finally the *maintenance phase*. Because every person is different, every business relationship is different. The way I am with Rick isn't the same way I am with John, another one of my investment partners. John doesn't always get my jokes, which bums me out sometimes, but that's okay. He's a different guy with a different personality.

Four Motivation Triggers; What Floats Their Boat?

Understanding what motivates people, especially your potential partners, can help you understand how to deepen and leverage your business relationships. It might surprise you to learn that not everyone in business is motivated by money, especially those with lots of it. For most affluent people it's no longer about the money. I didn't understand this concept when I first started out because I wasn't affluent. I thought everyone was motivated by the same thing in business, and the higher the return the more interested they would become.

As you grow and make more money and become more affluent, you step into accredited investor land (which I'm now in), and people pitch to you. "You can make twenty, twenty-two, even thirty percent return on your money!" My reaction is always, "So what? I can make that anywhere." In the position I'm now in, if someone is going to be successful pitching to me they have to connect with me. I have to feel I would be fulfilled somehow by being their partner. What is the mission? The deal has to have some emotional resonance with me.

That's why I harp so much about your brand. What makes you different? What's your distinct point of view, your alignment factors that you can share? The more affluent the people you're pitching to, the less rate of return matters. If you come to me and say, "You'll be able to make a great return, but even more than that we're committed to improving the lives of battered women by investing in safe houses, and here's how we're going to do it." That interests me because that moves me. That's a movement and a mission that I would align myself with and be a part of whether I make 5 percent or 25 percent. Motivation is a super-important concept.

We are not pitching institutions; we're pitching individuals. Private money partners are people first. I'm sitting across the table at La Loma drinking margaritas and eating chips and salsa with a person who doesn't have the same motivators as the next person. There are four psychological triggers that motivate a person. The first one is the friendship trigger. You bond over something more than just business. You'll find that there are some investment partners who are in it for the friendship. They're the people who say, "Hey, you want to go see a basketball game on Friday? Want to go grab a beer or a margarita?" If you don't think it's about friendship, what will happen the first time you say, "No, I have some other plans. Maybe catch me next time." ...Maybe there won't be a next time.

The second is the *consistency trigger*. Consistently do what you say you're going to do, and an investor might value that above all else. Remember to honor your commitments, big and small. If you say you're going to start at 9:00 a.m., start at 9:00 a.m., because people have expectations of you. Every single thing I tell my private money partner I'm going to do, I do. I honor all commitments, big and small, written and verbal. All that stuff has a cumulative effect on your partner. It leads to higher trust.

When they trust you, they'll give you more business. That is usually the time when they reveal that they have twice as much money available to you as they originally told you.

The third is the *reciprocity trigger*. The law of reciprocity is very powerful. Let's say you're relaxing at home at Christmastime and all of a sudden the doorbell rings and it's one of your neighbors. They've stopped by to give you an unexpected gift for Christmas.

You're like, "Oh crap." You don't have anything for them, and you feel like a total jerk. So you mumble, "Thank you so much," while you frantically look around the living room for something you can pass off as the gift you were going to give them but hadn't wrapped yet. Don't you hate that? That's the law of reciprocity in action. If somebody gives us something, it's like we're almost manic to do something for them in return. It's better to be the one bearing gifts, so use the reciprocity trigger to your advantage.

The fourth psychological trigger is the *belonging trigger*. People want to be part of a group or part of the family. That's why I love hanging out with my private money partners. It's a party. They're all working toward a common goal and supporting me. Because they're all supporting me, inadvertently they're all supporting each other, too, and they become friends as well. That's something I love being able to facilitate. Welcome people into the fold and make them feel they are important members.

Connecting with Your Partners

Communication is key. To successfully maintain and grow your relationships, you have to communicate regularly with your business partners, and not just when you need something. Doesn't it feel better when somebody just sits down with you and wants to talk or spend time without an agenda or some needy thing? Admittedly, the first couple of times you reach out to a private money partner without an agenda they're going to be suspicious. Usually no one wants to hang out with them unless they need something. They're going to assume you want to ask for more money. An awesome thing is going to happen at the end of that meeting when you stand up and say, "You know what? It was great spending time with you today. Thanks for hanging out," and you leave. They're going to be thinking, "Wow. That never happens."

Spending Time with Your Partners; Your New BFFs

So what can you do with your private money partners to connect on a personal level? Do anything that interests you both. You can go to a restaurant, or for a cup of coffee, or maybe a game of golf. A few of my private money partners are women, and I invite them to the salon for a pedicure. It's an opportunity to spend an hour together side by side in a relaxing environment and just chat about life, not about business. Maybe we'll read some of the trashy magazines they have in there and catch up on the gossip. "What is Jessica Simpson up to today? Can you believe Kim Kardashian did that?" It's a chance to deepen that relationship and make it more meaningful. There are tons of things you can do with your partners.

Here are some communication ideas: You can send out a quarterly newsletter to your investment partners and give them updates on what you're doing: "The project on Main Street is about three- quarters of the way there; we just laid the new foundation. We're ready to begin looking for our next opportunity. We're super- excited that so many of you want to come in on it with us."

Sending Cards and Gifts; The Hallmark Moments

Why not send your investment partners a personal letter with their monthly or quarterly payment? Don't just send them a check; send them birthday cards or investment anniversary cards. That's the kind of thing I love to do. You can send a gift or food basket on an important date. For big impact, I send a bottle of Dom Pérignon or Cristal. I'm big on fancy champagne because I think it's something they would never buy for themselves, and it's a big-impact gift.

Some wealthy investor friends of mine, Erin and Allen, just made the Inc. 500 list. It was a huge surprise for me to see their company on the list, so I immediately sent them a bottle of Cristal champagne.

Erin was pregnant, so she couldn't drink, but I just included a little note saying, "Congratulations on Inc. 500. So proud of you guys and so proud of the success you've achieved. Erin, sorry it's booze, but I know you guys will save it for a special occasion after the baby is born. Cheers. Love, Susan." They were so surprised and grateful, you would have thought I opened Fort Knox and got a brick of gold and trucked it to them. Do you think that the next time I have an investment opportunity and I need, say, $200,000 for a deal they will listen to what I have to say and likely invest with me? Absolutely!

You might be thinking that you don't have time to send out cards and remember your partners' significant dates. So automate the process with an online greeting card system like

SendOutCards. It's a system that allows you to send greeting cards via email. You choose a card, personalize it, choose the recipient, push a button, and send it off. You can send it to one person or to a whole group. You can add a gift, or not. Say you have ten investors who have all invested in a five-year project that closed on January 5th. You can go to SendOutCards.com, upload their names and addresses, choose a card, and set it to send a card to each investor every year on January 5th. It will even take a sample of your handwriting and use it to send personal messages as if you wrote them by hand. Pretty cool, huh? They also have a gift catalog. Along with the card you can choose to send baked goods, beverages, candy, baby gifts, kid gifts, men's gifts, pet gifts – all sorts of things. That's how I send out cookies and brownies and little surprises to my Getting the Money coaching students. To some of my coaching clients I send out a book called Five Years from Now. It's a beautiful hardcover gift book for writing out your five-year goals, and it's very cost effective.

What if you took a picture of a house that is for sale by owner, stuck it on a card, and sent it to the seller with "Sold" stamped across it? What kind of impact would that have? "Holy crap. That's my house on this card. Who is this person? Sold? Yes, I want to sell this house."

I sold a house one time and took a picture of the buyers sitting with big smiles at the closing table holding the keys to the house. Later I sent them a card with the picture I took and "I'd love to have your referrals" on the front. These are small gestures with big impact.

Using Social media to Manage Your Investors

Facebook and LinkedIn both allow you to form private groups through which you not only communicate with your investor members individually, but also allow your investors to communicate with each other. On LinkedIn it's called a members only group, and on Facebook it's called a closed or secret group. We have a private group for the Getting the Money program. Just visit GettingTheMoney.com for a link to join. On either platform you can share documents, add photos, and create events. "Registration is now open for the November Mastermind in San Diego. Click here to book your room." It's awesome for managing a group of investors. "Hey, everybody, look at the new foundation." Upload the picture. "Hey, everybody, just got the drywall done." Boom; post a picture of that. People are visual, so it's more impactful to post a picture than to send a written update or a newsletter.

It's very, very important to manage expectations. I think this is true in any relationship. I like to under-promise and then over-deliver. I want to let people know exactly what to expect so there's no confusion when we're working together. Everybody needs to be on the same page.

Are You Real?

Be a real person. We talked about this earlier, but so many people come up to me and say, "Oh my gosh. You're awesome. You're so real. The thing I love about you is that you're so real." When people tell me that I say, "What does that even mean? Of course I'm real." Somebody sent us an email that asked, "Is Susan Lassiter- Lyons even real?" So I took out my iPhone and shot a video. "Hi, I'm Susan Lassiter-Lyons, and I'm real. Look, here's my office. It's real. Look, there's Laura. She's real, too." When we posted it on our YouTube channel, it got over 1,200 views. So 1,200 people said, "Ooh, I want to know if Susan Lassiter-Lyons is real." Click. It's like *The Wizard of Oz* or something. "Pay no attention to the lady behind the giant machine!" My business might be larger than life, but I'm still just a chick who wears flip-flops and drinks margaritas.

When You Drop the Ball

Admit when you're wrong. If something goes wrong with your investment, the worst possible thing you can do is try to cover it up or not immediately tell your investment partners what's happening. The longer you try to go without being honest about what's going on, the worse it will get. I've learned that the hard way. When something goes wrong your mind jumps to, "Oh no, I'm going to miss this deadline. What am I going to do?" and you worry, worry, worry. You make yourself sick. Your mind automatically runs rampant with worse-case scenarios, even when they are completely ridiculous. "They're going to be upset with me. I'm not going to make a profit. They're never going to do a deal with me again. They're going to call the SEC. I'm going to jail."

But it's never as bad as you imagine. Years of dealing with banks has conditioned us to expect the worst when there is a payment default. But you're not dealing with banks; you're dealing with your partners. If you've treated them right, they're just as invested in helping you find a solution as you are. Have a conversation: "We ran into a snag. I made a mistake on the calculation. I needed a couple of thousand dollars more than I thought I needed. There's not going to be enough to make this month's payment. Can you just let the interest accrue and I'll take care of it at the end of the term when it pays off?" You'll hear, "Sure. Not a problem." Be transparent.

Party Fouls

Let's talk about business relationship mistakes – party fouls. Don't be that person at the party or the seminar who says, "Hi, my name is John. It's nice to meet you. Hey, I can get my hands on a great package of notes. Wanna take a look?" and shoves a phone in your face with pre-cued pictures glaring at you. My response is, "No. Can I get a cocktail first before you treat me like a sucker?" Those are the people I avoid like the plague. It's like they're always trying to sell you something.

My in-laws are on some anti-aging cream kick now. Every time they see me they chase me around with this anti-aging cream. I'm like, "Please get away from me. I'm not going to put that on my face! And I'm not going to buy it!" I end up avoiding them like the plague. Don't pitch too early or be uncomfortably persistent. If you can tell that somebody is not interested, just let it go.

Never sign somebody up without permission. Sometimes you make a mistake and give the wrong person your business card with your email address, and suddenly you're getting daily emails from a wholesaling schmo. If you're going to take someone's business card, ask them if it's okay to add them to your list.

Don't assume closeness. There are people who seem overly friendly right off the bat and just get in your grill. Don't be a close- talker – a space-invader. I hate that. Just be respectful.

Don't spam. Spammers are an infestation. Even worse are the people who pump out ridiculous numbers to snag the suckers. "I'm paying 19.4 percent interest for a $100,000 investment. Just contact me." I just got one of those on our Facebook page for an investment opportunity in Nigeria. Don't be a slimeball salesman. Respect the people who might become your partners.

First and foremost don't ignore your business relationships! Let this be a wake-up call. Set up SendOutCards and restart communication with your business contacts. Send an unexpected gift to a partner or someone who has helped you recently. Right here is where the rubber meets the road because if you befriend just one private money partner and treat them like gold, you'll have the ability and opportunity to make a lot of money for both of you without using a penny of your own. What's that worth to you?

Chapter Twelve

THE COMPLEXITY OF COMMITMENT

"If you think you can do a thing or think you can't do a thing, you're right."

−Henry Ford

"Do; There Is No Try"

Being committed to something isn't always easy; in fact, it can be complex in a lot of ways. We're going to go over something I call the "complexity of commitment." The framework of commitment is "do, study, master, and risk." When you are committed to something, you have to do it. You have to take some action. Les was a professional basketball player before he joined our Getting the Money coaching program. In order to become a basketball player, he had to get on the court and bounce the ball and put it in the basket as many times as possible. He couldn't just sit on his couch and say, "I bet if I stood there and shot it, I would score. Or if I got a little closer and I angled my hand like that, it might go in more times." He had to get out there and physically do the thing that he was committed to doing. He had to become a student of the game and study it. He had to learn the plays and techniques that would help him excel both offensively and defensively, and practice them again and again. The more time he spent on the hardwood, the better his game became.

Mastery; Becoming a Student of the Game

The next piece of the framework is mastery. In his book Outliers: the Story of Success, Malcolm Gladwell said that in order to master something you have to put in at least ten thousand hours doing that thing. Ten thousand hours. I started investing in real estate in 1994. I kept a log of my schedule, and I wrote about it in a blog post once called "The Biggest Lie You Tell Yourself." In that article I talk about how the biggest lie you tell yourself is that you don't have enough time to commit to something. People are always saying, "That sounds great, but I don't have the time to do it."

When I first started investing in real estate, I had a full-time job, a part-time job, and a forty-five-minute one-way commute each day. I also had no cash because I gave it all to the government after the options-investing debacle. I wasn't making much money. When I decided I wanted to leave Hertz in Park Ridge, New Jersey, I went back home to Colorado penniless. I had been in the car- rental industry for so long that that was my only skill set. When I started applying at places at the director level, I would get, "We're not hiring at that level," and I had to keep dumbing down my resume. First I would apply for director, then for manager, then for assistant. I wasn't getting any bites, and I think I'm a pretty good employee other than the whole flip-flop thing.

My sister worked at Pulte Mortgage, and she got me a job there in secondary marketing. I thought it was pretty cool because I was able to learn all about how mortgages work, how Wall Street works with mortgages, and why the rules are the rules. That was my full-time job. My part-time job was originating mortgages for my brother-in-law, Clifford, who was a mortgage broker in Pueblo. I would contact all my real estate investor friends and tell them I could hook them up with financing. Then I would write the loan, Clifford's company would close it, and I would make a commission. I was doing my real estate investing and driving forty-five minutes to work each morning and forty-five minutes home each night.

I committed myself to real estate investing, and, even more than that, I committed myself to starting my own mortgage company. I knew that all three jobs were going to help me achieve that goal. I knew I could leverage that experience and pull it off, and that's why I committed myself so completely. I logged all my hours for my full-time job, my part-time job, and the work I did on investing during every break. I turned my car into my loan origination office. I listened to motivational tapes like Tony Robins's telling me, "Who's the prize? You are the prize! Who's the prize? You are the prize!" I screamed it up and down the highway trying to psych myself up to get ready for another day to do what I had to do. On weekends I did my real estate investing.

When I decided to become a real estate investing trainer and coach, one of the questions people asked was, "What makes you think you have what it takes to stand up on the stage and teach real estate investing? What makes you such an expert?" So I counted up all the hours and it came to 22,400 hours. Since 1994 I have invested 22,400 hours honing the craft of real estate investing. That is a lot of time. It takes commitment to master anything. For me the result of that commitment was 26.2 million dollars in private money raised, involvement in 600 transactions, a five- to six-figure monthly cash flow, and a seven-figure net worth.

The point is that my success didn't happen overnight; I started at the beginning. I left Hertz broke with my tail between my legs. I had reached one of the highest levels in that company but ended up working in a cubicle as a marketing assistant at a mortgage company where I wasn't allowed to wear flip-flops or cook fish in the microwave (and that really peeved me). Obviously I couldn't stay there long. I was there because I didn't have any cash or any real credit to do what I wanted to do. I had to take what I could get in the spread on residential lease options. I worked and worked until I finally worked my way up to making about $1,600 a month in cash flow from my real estate investing business. That was my number.

Do you know what your number is for when you will quit your job? I wanted to do it when I hit $1,600. I look back on it now and wonder, "How could I have lived on $1,600?" I didn't have very many expenses back then, but I was super-scared. It was a risk.

No Risk, No Reward

Leaving my job to be a full-time investor was risky, and it felt scary. So I did what I usually do and prayed to God saying, "All right, Lord. Here is the thing. I feel like I've hit my number and now is the time that I should be quitting my job." Have you heard the John Burroughs quote "Leap and the net will appear"? I wanted to believe that so badly, but I just needed a little nudge. I said, "God if I am supposed to do real estate investing full time and this is the time that I am supposed to leave this job, give me a sign. You know me, so you have to make the sign completely obvious so I get it."

The furniture had been rearranged in our house and I hadn't noticed for weeks. All of a sudden one day I walked into the living room and said, "Didn't the couch used to be over there?"

I heard, "Yes, two weeks ago." Obviously I am not the most observant person, so I said, "Lord, give me a sign, and make it really obvious."

One day I left work and went downtown to have lunch with a friend. I was driving back to my office and thinking, "Lord, please just give me a sign. Give me a sign." I pulled up to a stop sign and right at that moment, in front of me in the crosswalk where I stopped, was an African American "little person." I'd never seen an African-American little person before. I watched as he walked in front of my car in the crosswalk, and then he turned and looked me right in the eye. He did a little parade wave and gave me a real big grin. I looked up and said, "Lord, thank you for the sign and thank you especially for making it so obvious that even I could see it." I drove right back down to the mortgage company, walked into my boss's office, and said, "I resign. I quit today." He was shocked. "What are you talking about? Why are you quitting today?" I paused and said, "It's a long story. I'll tell you someday over a margarita. I just know that it's time for me to go."

So I quit. And I leapt. I had my $1,600 a month, which was just enough to cover expenses. I didn't have any money for fun or entertainment or beer or food, which was an unfortunate miscalculation on my part. The net did appear, but in the form of a Texaco gas card. I had a Texaco food mart close to my house so I could use my Texaco gas card to buy fresh and nutritious food like Funyuns and Skittles. That was my Texaco-gas-card diet. They also had an ATM, and each month I would get sixty dollars in cash. That was my fun money for the whole month. It was not a lot, but I made it happen. I couldn't get a loan, so my only hope for investing was to use other people's money. They say that necessity is the mother of invention, and private money was my only choice.

I tried making my deals work with hard money, but there just wasn't enough profit for me. I started raising private money and decided I was going to be a rehabber, even though it didn't suit me. I didn't like it, had no interest in it, and wasn't very good at it, but it was where I saw the profits. For my very first deal, I had my private money partner lined up and all ready to go, but when clutch-time came, I backed out. I took that little weasel clause – the inspection clause – and said, "I found something, and I am out." It wasn't because I found anything wrong with the property; it was because I was scared of the risk. It was the very first time I was going to fund a deal using somebody else's money, and that was the scariest thing in the world to me. "What if something goes wrong? What if I lose their money? They are going to hate me, or worse. I can't do it." But everything in life is a risk. The one who takes the risk is the one who gets the reward.

When I lined up the next deal I said, "I am going to make this work!" It did, and it kept working. I went on to the next thing with private money – apartment buildings – and that worked. Then I became a hard-money lender, and that worked, too. I went from living on my gas card to being the manager of a three-and-a- half-million-dollar private equity mortgage pool in the span of eight years. It was because I was committed. I did it; I studied it; and I mastered it. You can, too.

Let's look at where you are right now. So far you've learned to create a business platform with several unique divisions. You've created a one-page business plan that includes a vision for your company and a succinct and effective value statement. You've learned where to find and how to identify private money prospects from three buckets: friends and family, people who are already investing in real estate, and people who are already making private loans to real estate investors. You've learned some marketing strategies for contacting prospects and piquing their interest in your business. You've learned how to structure the presentation and how to pitch the deal effectively to your private money prospects. We also talked about the right frame of mind and the right psychological space and mindset for understanding that you are the prize and that money is just a commodity. Finally, you've learned how to close the deal so you can get paid and move on to the next deal, and what it takes to commit yourself to succeed. You've come a long way, don't you think?

When I do my teaching events, I sometimes have a tendency to drop the content bomb. I just blanket everyone with content and see what sticks. My staff and I like to talk to attendees during breaks to see if we can pick up on themes that some or many of the attendees share. Often we find that there is something that keeps people from realizing their dreams. That's what this is all about, right? My dreams have already come true, so I'm in pay-it- forward mode in which I am committed to helping other people realize their dreams.

But I often find that people are dragging their feet. If that is you, you might have a "smart" problem. Smart people are great at worrying. Smart people are adept at conjuring up a dozen reasons to avoid taking action. It points to a fear of failure; you don't want to start unless you are 100 percent sure that you'll be successful. Does that sound like you? It's safer to analyze than to act because you get to stay in your safe place and you get to stay the smart one. But it's an illusion, because if you're in that place you'll never reach your true goal – your freedom goal. Remember the goal that you wrote down at the beginning of our journey together? That's the whole reason you're using real estate investing as your vehicle. That goal is your destination. You can't get there if you delay taking action because you always want to be 100 percent sure you're going to be successful before you start. If that's how you roll, then you might as well put down this book and go back to the daily grind of your other job, because nobody can ever be 100 percent sure of success at anything.

How often do you spend more time trying to figure out if something will work than you do taking action to see for yourself? "I just need one more course, and I'll be ready." "Let me just read one more book or watch one more DVD." "Let me just go to one more event and ask this one last question." I've heard it from so many people over the years: "Susan, I've gone to many boot camps, and I bought every single program. I've done coaching programs. I've done this, I've done that." I say, "How many deals have you done?" They say, "None." "Why not? What on Earth are yo waiting for??"

We create our own destiny. If you want to accomplish anything of note in your business, you have to start trusting. And the only one you have to start trusting is you. You have to trust yourself enough to know that when it comes right down to it, and you're in the midst of it and might not know the answer, at least you'll know where to go to get that answer.

Who Has Your Back?

I know we've talked about dreams – your dream destination and your dream investment plan that will magically transport you to that destination. Let me be blunt for a moment. Dreams don't come true. "What? Did Susan just write that?" They don't. Plans come true. Don't you agree? Maybe you were hoping that you could read a few books and attend a few lectures and then watch while investors beat a path to your door. But a dream without a plan is just a wish (Katherine Paterson); and hope is not a strategy (Dr. Benjamin Ola Akande). So what's your plan? When you need help tweaking that plan, who is going to help you? The plan starts with support. The plan starts with surrounding yourself with people who have been there and done that, and with mentoring and coaching. Here's what I know for sure: There is enough information in this book for you to take the leap and start putting together deals with private money. I also know that you can start right now, and you can do it!

Remember, I was exactly where you are now. I wanted to accomplish something, achieve something, and master something in my business, but I felt like I needed some help. I needed some guidance and I needed to know that somebody had my back. When I went right to the edge and needed to leap off and take that risk, I was scared and wished to God I had somebody right there with me. Isn't that really what we all want? The difference is that nobody had my back until I started doing it. I still work with a coach because when I need help with my business I want to know that there's somebody I can call or email to give me an honest answer. I need someone to kick me in the tail when I need it, motivate me when I stumble, and catch me when I fall.

I didn't have the courses, coaches, websites, and webinars that would have made the first few years smoother and far less stressful, but you do. If all you need is a little more support and a little more encouragement to kick your business into high gear, I am offering you a solution. I have many programs. I have individual coaching programs and group coaching programs. I have Facebook groups and I have LinkedIn groups. I have webinars and I do seminars. I have programs to help newbies and programs to help multi- million-dollar investors. There is power in support.

I would like you to think about two final points. First, the very worst thing you can do at this point is nothing. I just gave you the keys to the car. All you need to do now is start driving. If you walk away, with the keys in hand, you'll be quitting on yourself.

The second thing I want you to think about is the first step of the commitment framework: do. Start doing. If you need support, fine; I have a hundred ways to support you. At some point, though, you will need to put the car in drive and start heading to your dream destination. The time to start is now.

Your call to action is this: Grab your flip-flops, pour a margarita, go to my website at gettingthemoney.com, and join us. If you need help taking that first step, I will help you. If you have taken that step and need support or want to have some questions answered, I will help you. If you are successful with this program but you want to know how to move to a multi-million-dollar level, I will help you. Together we can do this!

I want to thank you for taking this journey with me, and I hope with all my heart you take what you've learned to translate the reality of your dreams into your ordinary day for extraordinary results. Cheers!

CASE STUDIES FROM STUDENTS WHO USED THE INFORMATION IN THIS BOOK TO SUCCEED

SHAE BYNES

Shae Bynes and her husband were "buy and hold" investors and had already purchased their first property when they met Susan. They had a rental property but wanted to grow their portfolio, and were not sure how to go outside of the traditional bank route. Susan was teaching at the time, and Shae was able to join a webinar Susan offered. Shae believed that Susan could help her move her business to the next level and knew that the program Susan taught would work, but she wasn't sure it would work for her. Shae didn't know anyone with money and thought maybe she was too new in real estate investing for investors to want to work with her. She battled with many of the same concerns all newbies share.

Shae trusted Susan and her team and knew they were telling the truth about the program and about how they kept saying she just needed to get out there and do it. Shae had never let self-doubt stop her before, so she just moved forward with no clue whether it was going to work for her or not. She trusted herself to know that if she did make some screw-ups she could fix them along the way.

Soon Shae was successful in bringing four investors on board and was able to use the $400,000 in private money to fund multiple deals with many different people. She said, "That's the beauty of this. Once you've done a deal with someone and they see you make it something that's a win for both of you, they're asking, "What else do you have?" They see better returns with you than they see with the stock market and other places where they have their money."

It wasn't easy at first. For a long time Shae worried that she couldn't make this program work without a warm market – friends and family who had money. She didn't know who to talk to and didn't know what she was going to do. But she knew she needed to start somewhere and take action. She began by simply talking to people. She shared her ideas about the deals she wanted to do and then practiced pitching presentations to her friends and family. When she realized that people were receptive to what she had to say, it gave her the confidence to put real deals in front of people who could do something with them. That's when the magic started to happen. Shae said, "This stuff works but you've got to work it, and you're going to build your confidence in it by actually taking action."

Shae recalled that taking action was something Susan was always encouraging people to do. Even with all her self-doubts, Shae simply needed to start doing it to get things rolling. "I get this question all the time: 'Does it work? Does it work? Does it work?' The answer is 'Yes, it works; but only if you work.' It doesn't work by itself. You have to be willing to deal with the challenges. You have to be willing to deal with the inevitable no's that you're going to get. You have to be willing to deal with the hard questions that you don't know the answers to in the beginning. You have to go through that to get to the other side, and the other side is sweet."

After taking Susan's webinar and gaining the confidence to take action, Shae has not looked back. She says the focus on real estate has been on the buy-and-hold side over the past few years, and they have converted some of the properties they were holding as landlords into lease options. Then they sold them off and held the notes on them. "We have kind of a mix of things going on, but private money was the key for all of it to take place. It has been very profitable." Shay admits that it has not been a cakewalk, and that real estate investing has its challenges; but in the end there has been more good than bad. The program itself is great financially. People can make money using all the different real estate investment strategies. "Real estate investing is just one of those things that is an absolute; it's a wealth generator, and it's something that's important not just for me and my husband, but for our kids. We have two kids, and we want to have something with a longer-lasting impact than the two of us. Real estate investing provides that." For Shae and her husband, the journey has taught them skills that translate outside of the investment world. They learned about negotiations, how to create and operate with large budgets, and how to manage people. These insights have a wide range of applications for any entrepreneur in almost any business setting.

Shae recommends Susan for training at any level. "Susan is really one of the best teachers of real estate investing that I've ever learned from in all my years of getting training on real estate investing. She is thorough, and she is of high integrity. A lot of times in this business you run into people who are just not operating with your best in mind. That's something that you never have to worry about with Susan; just high, high integrity."

Shae Bynes is a private money real estate investor and co-founder of Kingdom Driven Entrepreneur, an online community for "Entrepreneurs of faith" at KingdomDrivenEntrepreneur.com.

GREG GREENWOOD

Greg Greenwood has been around real estate for the past twenty- five years. He owns a construction company that specializes in custom home-building and remodeling. Through the years Greg had opportunities to flip a few houses, but had never looked at real estate investing as a business. About two years ago Greg decided to look into expanding what he was doing. The construction industry had just come through a tough four or five years that reinforced for him the need to create some residual opportunities or look at diversifying his income in some way. As close as he was to the industry, he never really looked at real estate as the answer.

One day Greg came across something that Susan had posted about real estate investing. Greg liked her style and approach, liked what she was about, and liked her presentation enough that he decided to jump on board. He started following what Susan was saying and began to use her as his go-to person for learning the process. He put himself in an information-gathering mode and spent the next year learning. "I wasn't really going to act on anything for the first year because I was in that realm of 'I don't know what I don't know.'"

Every time he turned over another stone he was amazed and excited. Because he didn't know what was out there, he didn't know which real estate investing path would be best for him. Greg used the time to establish his new investment business, set up his website, and investigate what it would take to be successful. He dove into Susan's program and learned the techniques and processes she was teaching. "All of the things that Susan talks about, from going to the REIA and meeting people to letting everybody you talk to know what it is you're doing – I lived that, and I still do today."

As it relates to private money and the raising of private money, Greg thinks he was somewhat blessed. He was not afraid to talk to people, and the people he had the opportunity to talk to all seemed to have a lot of money. Everyone, including both his past and present clients, knew that in addition to construction he was also investing in real estate. "I let everyone know that my business had changed from being a construction company to a real estate investment and development company. Construction is a leg of that, and people recognize that they have some opportunities to participate with me."

To date, Greg has raised $3.5 million in committed private money, but says there is as much as $20 million available for the right deals. "If I can put the deals together, the money is going to be there for them." He recognizes that people who go out and get the deals before they get the money to fund them will have a difficult time. Saying "If you have a deal, the money just comes" is not always true because of the timelines associated with the deals. "Money doesn't just fall out of the sky. If you share with people what it is you're doing and what the deal is that you're putting together, and you can get those people excited about it, it's the concept of the deal that will make people want to participate. Then you just set up the structure for that to happen."

Of all the concepts Greg has learned about private money real estate investing, mindset is among the most important. He found that when people in his position approached a potential investor about money, they felt like they were asking to borrow money, and nobody likes to ask for money. But you should never feel ashamed about asking for what you want to do. Instead you should feel like you have the greatest thing in the world and you would feel embarrassed or ashamed if you kept it to yourself. You should want to share it with everybody you know.

"If that's the attitude you have when you share the opportunity, people are going to relate to it, like, "Wow, this really is great, and I want to be a part of it!" He found that all you need to do is share the possibility of an opportunity with somebody else and let that person decide for themselves. "You're not going to try to persuade them. You're just putting yourself in front of them and then they make their own decisions." Greg contends that because they're a professional, they will do what they need to do. If you have that mindset, passion, and excitement, and show you're committed to what you're doing, people will want to participate. Coming in with the right mindset will blow away a lot of the fears that people have of being rejected. When you're not looking for them to give you money, there is no rejection. It's all about the mindset.

When asked how Susan's approach and teachings influenced his business, Greg had this to say: "Susan is probably the most influential person in my real estate learning – as a person, and in terms of her grasp of all of the techniques. That's something I love about her, too; she's very, very savvy in all the ways of investing. I think that lends itself to being successful in this business. You don't have to be doing all the techniques, and you don't have to be excellent at all the techniques, but it's great to have them in your bag of tricks if you need to pull one out to close a deal."

Greg Greenwood is the owner of a real estate investment and development company. His website at www.bluelabelproperties. com focuses on buying houses in the San Fernando Valley of Los Angeles.

BRENDEN KANAKAOLE

Brenden Kanakaole was brand new to real estate investing. Business was not good for this Hawaiian-born investor; he had no money to fund deals and no confidence to approach people. Something about Susan grabbed his attention, so he signed up for a few of her courses. Brenden was blown away not just by the content but by the inspiration that Susan gave him. "I didn't even know her, but I felt if I could just be a part of her coaching program, I could break barriers in my business."

Brenden was right. He recently purchased a large house in his home town of Waipahu, Hawaii, that he plans to fix and flip. Just last week he raised an additional $135,000 for his business and is now participating in a joint venture on a multi-family property in Texas. "My partner in this Texas joint venture needed some help establishing some deal-flow channels, so I was happy to use the knowledge I learned from Susan." Susan's program helped give Brenden the tools he needed and the confidence he lacked to present his ideas to his new private money partner. "I had known this person for years, but I never had the confidence to approach him for private money." Brenden will receive 50 percent of the equity and cash flow for the Texas multi-family property, and has access to funds totaling $1 million. "I originally pitched him on my Hawaii business, but he was not interested. He later said that he wanted to invest with me, but just not in Hawaii." Who was the prize? Brenden was the prize!

Things are taking off for Brenden, but it wasn't without a little sweat. "Be ready to work!" he warns. "You can't be passive about this stuff." He also had to figure out what strengths he had working for him in his business. He was fortunate in that he either personally knew some people with money or was able to network with the right people from clubs and associations to fill up his three buckets. Because he had two jobs, it was harder for Brenden to develop his social media marketing strategies – his website, Facebook page, and LinkedIn page – than it was to raise private money!

Brenden's business has turned around, and he was happy to share his thoughts about Susan and her team: "Susan's company is unique in that they are not just real estate coaches, but life coaches as well. She has helped bring life to my business and has given me the courage to talk to people." He went on to say, "She was blunt, but I respect that because she walks the walk and talks the talk in a really great way. My wife has more confidence in me, as well as my partners." The program itself was challenging, but through it Brenden found a rhythm that he maintains even today. "I just don't want to stop. My weeks are busy, but I've been striving to make one or two private money presentations a week."

Brenden Kanakaole is currently working and living in Hawaii where he is a member of Hawaii Real Estate Investors (HREI).

ABOUT
SUSAN LASSITER-LYONS

Susan's been an entrepreneur all her life. In fact, she started three businesses before she was thirteen years old.

Susan was a national sales trainer and revenue manager for a Fortune 100 company. Translation: She was on the road three weeks a month in an ultra-corporate environment that sucked, mainly because she wasn't allowed to wear flip-flops to work. (Susan really loves flip-flops.)

She left that corporate gig in 1998, and after brief stints at a few companies to learn, opened her own mortgage company in 2000. For eight years things went great. Susan's company was the number-one mortgage company in Denver specializing in residential, commercial, and private funding specifically for real estate investors. She participated in more than 600 real estate transactions and created a private equity mortgage hedge fund raising 26.2 million dollars.

When the 2008 real estate crisis hit, Susan took her knowledge online and created the Lassiter Publishing Group, offering digital information and business transformation. Her work creates lasting, profitable outcomes for more than 9,000 customers and 45,000 global subscribers.

Lassiter Publishing Group specializes in developing, publishing, and marketing courses and coaching programs for real estate investors and other independent investors seeking financial freedom. Susan is the Chief Fun Officer of Lassiter Publishing Group, whose company mission statement is "Have fun. Create value." And she wears flip-flops almost every day.

ABOUT
SUSAN LASSITER-LYONS

Susan teaches real estate investors how to raise capital.

And then she can help you grow, scale, and optimize.

She is the founder and creator of Getting the Money: The Simple System for Raising Private Money for Real Estate. To date, her students have cumulatively raised more than $500 million in private money for real estate using the concepts she teaches in her course and coaching.

Connect with Susan and discover how she can help you at: GettingTheMoney.com

Made in the USA
Coppell, TX
21 September 2020

38387291R00085